The Rich and the Poor

A Book to Change Your Financial Life

Cristian Pontes

I dedicate this work to all those who have the desire to achieve a better life and who wish to contribute to making the world a more just and equitable place. I hope this book can be a source of inspiration and change for those who read it, offering clarity and wisdom in making decisions about investments, entrepreneurship, and strategies for overcoming the challenges of such an unpredictable and hostile world. My goal is to provide valuable and practical information that helps people achieve their financial and personal goals while contributing to a better world. May this work be a guide for those seeking prosperity and fulfillment, while making a difference in the lives of those around them.
Cristian Pontes
Youtube Programa Chris Tattoo

Contents

The Rich and the Poor
A Book to Change Your Financial Life

Introduction

Welcome to a journey of financial empowerment and abundance! In this book, we will explore the keys to unlocking the doors of poverty and creating a life of wealth. It's not just about making more money; it's about cultivating a mindset of abundance, learning to be resourceful, and making the most of what you have. We will delve into practical strategies like saving money, cutting unnecessary expenses, and changing habits to build a solid financial foundation. We will also address the importance of surrounding yourself with prosperous people and the power of investing wisely. But it's not just about the mechanics of money - it's also about overcoming limiting beliefs, pushing limits, and facing fears to take risks and achieve success. And as we grow and prosper, we will explore how to pass these lessons on to future generations and maintain prosperity in our families.

The stories presented covered various topics related to personal and business finance. Some highlighted the importance of personal development, overcoming limits and limiting beliefs, as well as creating a wealth mindset and the importance of financial literacy from childhood. Other stories addressed the successes and failures of great entrepreneurs in business, reinforcing the importance of effective financial management. Bankruptcy cases resulting from financial mismanagement were also explored, emphasizing the need to take calculated risks to achieve success. Finally, one account highlighted the importance of philanthropy and maintaining prosperity in the family. All of these examples illustrate the relevance of sound financial education and responsible financial management in achieving success and financial security.

Are you ready to embark on this journey of abundance and possibility? Let's get started!

Chapter 1

Winning the Lottery

Many years ago, in a small town called Piranguinho in the interior of Brazil, lived a man named José. José worked hard every day in a peanut brittle factory, but his salary was so low that he could barely support his family of five children. Despite the difficulties, he always maintained the hope of one day being able to provide a better life for his family.

One day, while buying his lottery ticket, José could not imagine that his life would change forever. That night, he hit the lucky numbers and became a millionaire overnight. From that moment on, everything changed.

After winning the lottery, the poor man's life changed completely. He no longer had to worry about money and could finally indulge in all his luxuries and desires. He bought a luxurious house, sports cars, designer clothes, and began frequenting the most exclusive places in town. He felt superior to everyone around him and began to humiliate those he considered inferior. José began to spend money without worrying about the future. He enjoyed flaunting his wealth and humiliating all the people around him, judging them as inferior.

His longtime friends, who had helped him in difficult times, noticed the change in his behavior and began to distance themselves. He didn't care, as he thought they were envious of his new life of wealth. He also began to distance himself from his family, thinking they were a burden in his new life of luxury.

The poor man spent money on frivolous and expensive things without thinking about the future. He did not know how to manage his money properly and soon began to accumulate debts. He thought he could continue spending without consequences, as he had a lot of money in his bank account. However, his debts soon exceeded the value of his fortune.

When his creditors started calling, he realized that he could no longer maintain his extravagant lifestyle. He became desperate and tried to borrow money to pay his debts, but no one wanted to lend to him after seeing his financial situation. He lost everything he had won in the lottery and was even poorer than before.

Without friends or family to help him, he was alone in his sadness and regret. He realized that his ruin was caused by his lack of financial education, selfishness, and lack of love for others. He never cared about those who helped him in the past and now he was paying the price for his arrogance and ignorance.

The poor man realized that true wealth does not come from money or material possessions, but from those who surround us and love us. He promised himself that he would change his life and focus on the things that really matter. He learned the hardest lesson of his life and now hopes to regain the trust of those who love him and deserve his respect.

From that moment on, he promised to be more humble and help those in need, so that no one else has to go through the same painful path that he did. He began working hard again, but this time with the intention of saving and investing in a better future for his family and himself.

The story of the poor man who won the lottery and lost everything serves as a reminder that money cannot buy happiness or true friends. True wealth comes from the love, respect, and gratitude we have for others. The man learned this lesson the hard way, but we hope that others can learn from his story and avoid making the same mistakes.

The best use of money after winning the lottery can vary

according to each person's needs and goals. In José's case, he would have to worry about his family's well-being and preserve his assets as an inheritance for his children. However, there are some suggestions that can help ensure a more responsible and beneficial use of the money:

1. Paying off debts: It is important to pay off all outstanding debts, avoiding interest and fines, and ensuring greater financial peace of mind in the future.

Paying off debts is one of the first things that should be done when receiving an unexpected amount of money, such as winning the lottery. This is an action that can bring many benefits to the individual's financial life, and that is often neglected in favor of frivolous expenses.

The payment of outstanding debts is essential for maintaining a healthy financial life. When you have debts, it is common to pay interest and fines, which can make the situation even more difficult to reverse. In addition, the accumulation of debts can lead to a series of problems, such as increased indebtedness and loss of financial credibility.

By paying off outstanding debts, the individual can get rid of a great financial burden, and gain a clearer view of their current financial situation. With fewer debts to pay, it is possible to direct resources to other areas of life, such as investments and essential expenses such as food and housing.

Paying off debts can also help improve the individual's credit score. This is because by paying off debts, the individual's name is removed from the list of defaulters, which increases their financial credibility with financial institutions. With this, it is possible to have access to better loan and financing conditions in the future.

Another important point is that paying off debts can help the individual avoid the debt cycle. When you have many debts, it is common to resort to loans to pay them off. However, this practice can lead to an even greater accumulation of debts, which can become a vicious cycle difficult to break.

Finally, it is important to highlight that paying off debts brings a sense of relief and financial peace of mind. When you have many outstanding debts, it is common to feel a great pressure and concern about the future. By paying off debts, the individual can have a greater sense of security and financial stability.

Paying off debts is one of the best ways to use an unexpected amount of money, such as a lottery prize. In addition to ensuring greater financial peace of mind in the future, this attitude can help avoid the debt cycle, improve credit score, and bring a sense of relief and emotional well-being. Therefore, it is important to prioritize debt repayment before directing resources to other areas of life.

2. Investing in education and personal development: Taking courses, specializations, and improvements can improve the career and open up new business and investment opportunities.

Investing in education and personal development is one of the most intelligent and profitable ways to apply money. After all, education is an investment that never loses value and can bring numerous benefits to personal and professional life.

By qualifying with courses and specializations, it is possible to improve the career, gain new job opportunities, and increase the salary. In addition, the knowledge acquired can be applied to your own business or financial investments.

There are several options for courses and specializations, from the most basic to the most advanced. It is possible to study in person or online, according to the availability of time and financial resources. And for those who want an even more in-depth learning, there are options for master's and doctoral degrees in various areas of knowledge.

In addition to technical courses and specializations, it is also important to invest in personal development. This includes activities that stimulate creativity, communication, leadership, and emotional intelligence, for example. These skills are valued in various sectors and can make a difference when it comes to getting a job or a promotion.

It is important to remember that investment in education and personal development is not an immediate thing, but rather a long-term one. It takes patience and persistence to reap the rewards of this investment. However, it is a safe path to building a solid career and a more financially stable life.

Investing in education and personal development is one of the best ways to apply money in an intelligent and profitable manner. In addition to bringing benefits to one's career and personal life, the knowledge acquired can be applied to one's own business or financial investments. Therefore, it is an investment worth making that can yield long-term results.

3. Investing in businesses: one can invest in their own business or an existing enterprise, helping to create jobs and contributing to the local economy.

Investing in businesses can be a viable option for those who want to make their money work for them. In addition to being a way to increase personal wealth, investing in businesses can contribute to local economic development, creating jobs and boosting the economy.

One way to invest in businesses is through the creation of one's own enterprise. This option requires some knowledge about business management, the market, and finance, but can be very rewarding and profitable in the long term. Before starting a business, it is important to conduct market research to identify opportunities and potential obstacles. It is also necessary to have a well-structured business plan that includes the stages of the enterprise, short-term, medium-term, and long-term goals and objectives.

For those who wish to invest in existing businesses, there are various options in the market, such as buying shares of companies on the stock exchange, investing in real estate investment funds, or participating in crowdfunding for startups. Each option requires a certain degree of knowledge and market analysis.

In addition to contributing to job creation and local economic development, investing in businesses can bring financial benefits to the investor. It is important to remember, however, that investments in businesses are generally medium to long term, which requires patience and dedication to achieve the expected results. It is also necessary to bear in mind that, like any investment, there are risks involved and the possibility of losing part or all of the invested capital.

Another option for investing in businesses is by supporting local microentrepreneurs. This option not only helps to boost the local economy but also contributes to improving the quality of life of the entrepreneurs and their families. Often, a small investment can make a big difference in the life of an entrepreneur and help them leverage their business.

Investing in businesses can be an excellent option for those who want to increase their wealth and contribute to the local economy. However, it is important to remember that investments in businesses require a certain degree of knowledge and market analysis. It is also essential to remember that every investment involves risks and that it is important to have a solid financial plan and well-defined strategies before investing in any type of business.

4. Investing in real estate: acquiring a property of one's own can be an advantageous option to avoid rental expenses and ensure long-term wealth.

Investing in real estate is an option that many people consider when thinking about long-term investments. Owning a property can bring several advantages, such as financial security, stability, and the possibility of having a solid and valuable asset.

One of the main advantages of investing in real estate is avoiding rental costs. When you own a property, you do not have to bear the costs of rent, which are often high and can significantly compromise the budget. Moreover, investing in a property of your own is a way to have a long-term housing guarantee, which brings stability and peace of mind for the investor.

Another advantage of investing in real estate is the possibility of asset appreciation. By acquiring a property in a valued location, its value may increase over time, generating profit for the investor. Additionally, investing in real estate can also bring financial returns through rentals, when the property is put up for lease.

It is worth noting that investing in real estate can also bring disadvantages. One of the main challenges is the initial investment value, which is often high and may be difficult to afford. Furthermore, the purchase of a property may involve several additional costs, such as registration fees, taxes, maintenance, and renovations.

Another important point to consider is that the real estate market is influenced by various external factors, such as the economy, politics, and social changes. Therefore, it is important to exercise caution and conduct a careful analysis before investing in a property.

It is also necessary to consider that, as with any other type of investment, it is necessary to conduct market research and choose a property that meets the investor's needs and has potential for appreciation. Additionally, having a good negotiation strategy and relying on the assistance of a specialized professional can help avoid possible traps or errors.

Investing in real estate can be a advantageous and profitable option for those seeking long-term financial stability. However, it is necessary to carefully evaluate the advantages and disadvantages, costs, and risks involved before making the decision to invest. With a good market analysis and a well-defined strategy, it is possible to make a solid and safe investment in real estate.

5. Contributing to social causes: donating part of the money to social causes or non-profit organizations can help improve the lives of others and contribute to a better world.

When a person earns a significant amount of money, one of the options is to contribute to social causes or non-profit organizations. This is a way to use the money to make a difference in the lives of others and contribute to the building of a fairer and more equal society.

There are several social causes that deserve attention and financial support, such as the fight against hunger and poverty, environmental protection, promotion of education, health, and well-being, among others. Additionally, there are several non-profit organizations that work with these causes and have experience and capacity to make good use of donated money.

When contributing to social causes, the person can choose those that best align with their personal values and goals. It is important to research and evaluate the organizations before making a donation, verifying their transparency, reputation, and social impact.

One of the advantages of contributing to social causes is the personal satisfaction it can bring. Knowing that the money is being used to make a difference in the lives of others and to improve society can be very gratifying and rewarding. Additionally, the person can become an example and inspiration for others to do the same.

Another advantage is that donations to social causes can have tax benefits in some countries. In some cases, donations can be deducted from income tax, which means that the person can pay less taxes at the end of the year. This can be an additional advantage for those who want to make a difference and save money at the same time.

However, it is important to remember that contributing to social causes does not mean abandoning personal financial responsibility. It is necessary to balance support for causes with personal financial planning, to ensure that basic expenses and financial commitments are met.

Finally, contributing to social causes is an important way to use money to improve the lives of others and contribute to a better world. It is an option that should be considered by all people who want to make a difference and leave a positive legacy for future generations.

It is important to remember that, regardless of the chosen use, it is essential to maintain proper financial planning and not spend beyond one's means. Consulting a finance professional can also be a good option to ensure responsible and beneficial use of the money earned in the lottery.

Chapter 2

Understanding Poverty and Wealth

One of the most inspiring examples of how it is possible to overcome poverty and achieve wealth is the story of Oprah Winfrey, one of the richest and most influential women in the world. Oprah was born in 1954 in a poor family in Mississippi, United States. Her mother was single and often struggled to take care of Oprah and her siblings.

As a child, Oprah went through several difficulties and even traumas, including sexual abuse by a relative. However, she found refuge in education and religion. At 14, she moved in with her father in Nashville, Tennessee, where she began working at a local radio station as a news anchor.

Oprah quickly stood out and, at 19, was hired as a television show host in Baltimore. Her ability to interview and connect with people made her popular and, in 1983, she moved to Chicago to host "AM Chicago", which was later renamed "The Oprah Winfrey Show".

The show became a success and, in no time, Oprah became one of the most influential women in American television. She used her platform to address social and political issues, as well as to promote self-help and personal development.

Oprah also began expanding her business into other areas, including her own television network, the Oprah Winfrey Network, and her own line of products, including books, clothing, and beauty products.

Today, Oprah is one of the richest women in the world, with a net worth estimated at over $2 billion. She is known for her philanthropy, having donated millions of dollars to charities and social causes.

The story of Oprah Winfrey is an inspiring example of how it is possible to overcome adversity and achieve wealth through education, hard work, and perseverance. Her story also demonstrates the power of determination and belief in oneself, regardless of the circumstances in which one is born.

On the opposite side of the spectrum, there are several accounts of people who have gone from a life of wealth to poverty, often due to financial problems or changes in the job market.

An example is the case of Brazilian soccer player Ronaldinho Gaúcho. Known as one of the best players in the world, Ronaldinho accumulated a great fortune throughout his career, with multimillion-dollar contracts with top clubs and sponsorships. He also had investments in real estate, cars, and other properties.

However, in 2019, Ronaldinho was arrested in Paraguay along with his brother for entering the country with fake documents. From then on, his financial situation began to change. To pay for bail and lawyer expenses, he had to sell several properties, including a mansion in Porto Alegre valued at around R$ 7 million.

Moreover, Ronaldinho faced problems with his companies and businesses. His watch brand, for instance, went bankrupt and left million-dollar debts. As a result, his fortune began to significantly decrease.

Currently, Ronaldinho faces a difficult financial situation and lives in a hotel in Rio de Janeiro, after having his passport seized by the Brazilian government due to tax debts. He still faces legal proceedings and tries to recover his financial situation, but the decline in his fortune is an example of how even extremely rich people can go through financial difficulties.

To better understand the concept of wealth and poverty, we will divide this topic into 5 different aspects.

1. Income disparity: one of the main differences between poverty and wealth is income. People in poverty often have low and limited income, which makes it difficult to access basic needs such as food, housing, and healthcare. Meanwhile, wealthy people have high income and often have access to luxuries such as cars, luxurious homes, and trips abroad.

Income disparity is one of the main factors contributing to social disparity between poverty and wealth. While people in poverty often struggle to meet their basic needs such as food, housing, and healthcare, wealthy people have access to luxuries and comforts that are often considered superfluous.

Income is a determining factor for a person's financial well-being. People in poverty have limited income and often depend on government social assistance programs to survive. This means they have fewer choices when it comes to food, housing, and healthcare. They may have to opt for less nutritious foods or live in poor conditions because they don't have the financial resources to make better choices.

On the other hand, wealthy people have access to financial resources that allow them to make more informed and luxurious choices. They can choose where to live, where to travel, and where to invest. They have access to high-quality healthcare and can afford expensive services such as specialized medical treatments or cosmetic surgeries.

Additionally, wealthy people have the option to invest their money in assets that provide them with passive income, such as real estate or stock investments. This allows them to further increase their wealth and maintain a comfortable lifestyle over time.

On the other hand, people in poverty often don't have access to these investment options and may struggle to build long-term wealth. Income disparity also affects social mobility. Wealthy people often have access to better educational and professional opportunities, allowing them to move up the social ladder. People in poverty, on the other hand, often don't have access to these same opportunities and may have difficulty escaping poverty.

In conclusion, income disparity is one of the main differences between poverty and wealth. The limited income of people living in poverty often deprives them of access to basic necessities and restricts their options for investment and social mobility. Meanwhile, wealthy individuals have access to luxuries and opportunities that allow them to build wealth and maintain a comfortable lifestyle.

2. Access to education: Education is one of the main ways to escape poverty and pursue a more prosperous life. Unfortunately, many people living in poverty do not have access to quality education, while wealthy individuals often have access to prestigious schools and universities, giving them greater opportunities for professional and financial growth.

Education is a powerful tool for transforming people's lives and enabling social mobility. Unfortunately, the lack of access to education is a reality that affects many people living in poverty, making it even more difficult to pursue a more prosperous life.

Education is one of the main means of acquiring skills and knowledge that are essential for personal and professional development. However, people living in poverty often lack access to quality schools, adequate teaching materials, and trained teachers, which limits their chances of obtaining quality education and consequently better job and income opportunities. On the other hand, wealthy individuals often have access to prestigious schools and universities that offer high-quality education, as well as a wide range of resources and networking opportunities. This means that they have a significant advantage over people living in poverty, as they can acquire skills and knowledge that allow them to enter high-level professions and earn higher salaries.

Furthermore, the lack of access to education can perpetuate a vicious cycle of poverty and social marginalization. Without quality education, people have difficulty obtaining jobs that allow them to support themselves and their families, which leads to a cycle of poverty and social exclusion.

On the other hand, education can help break this cycle and offer an opportunity for change. When people have access to quality education, they can develop skills and knowledge that allow them to pursue new job opportunities and advance in their careers. Additionally, quality education can help promote social inclusion, giving people living in poverty an opportunity to fully participate in society and have an active voice in their community.

It is important to note that the lack of access to education is not only a problem in developing countries. Even in wealthy countries, people living in poverty often face barriers to accessing quality education. For example, schools located in low-income areas often have fewer resources and fewer trained teachers than schools in wealthier areas.

Access to education is crucial for people to escape poverty and pursue a more prosperous life. Education can help develop essential skills and knowledge for personal and professional success, promote social inclusion, and offer an opportunity for change. It is essential that measures be taken to ensure that all people have access to quality education, regardless of their income or geographical location.

3. Level of health: People living in poverty often lack access to adequate health services, which can result in more serious health problems and even premature death. Wealthy individuals, on the other hand, have access to high-quality medical care, allowing them to maintain good health and quality of life.

Health is one of the most precious assets of human beings, and having access to quality medical care is essential to ensuring health and well-being. Unfortunately, not all people have access to the same healthcare resources, and income inequality is one of the main factors that influence the quality of medical care received.

People in poverty often face difficulties in accessing adequate healthcare services. This can result from a lack of financial resources to pay for medical treatments or a lack of access to hospitals and clinics in their communities. Often, these individuals end up suffering from more serious health problems and even premature death because they cannot obtain the necessary treatment.

Moreover, the lack of access to adequate healthcare can also lead to a range of poverty-related health problems, such as chronic diseases, dental and nutritional problems, and infectious diseases. These issues are more common in poor communities and can significantly affect the quality of life.

On the other hand, wealthy people have access to high-quality medical care. They can afford to pay for private health insurance plans and have access to top-tier hospitals and clinics. Moreover, they also have more financial resources to pay for advanced medical treatments such as surgeries and intensive therapies when necessary.

This means that wealthy people have a higher life expectancy and a better overall quality of life. They have more chances to recover from illnesses and injuries, allowing them to continue working and enjoying life. Additionally, they also have fewer poverty-related health problems, such as dental and nutritional issues.

The difference in access to healthcare between rich and poor people is one of the main reasons why social inequality is such a big problem in many parts of the world. When people do not have access to quality medical care, they are at a higher risk of suffering from serious illnesses and injuries, which can lead to a range of other social and economic problems.

To address this inequality, it is important to make a continuous effort to improve access to healthcare in poor communities. This can involve building more hospitals and clinics in deprived areas, as well as creating programs that make healthcare services more accessible and affordable. Additionally, it is also important to make efforts to educate people about the importance of health and medical care, encouraging them to seek treatment when necessary.

The difference in access to healthcare between rich and poor people is one of the main ways in which social inequality is perpetuated in many parts of the world. It is important to make efforts to improve access to healthcare in deprived communities, ensuring that all people can have access to quality medical care, regardless of their income.

4. Social environment: People in poverty often live in high-crime and violent areas with little access to safe and community public spaces. Wealthy people generally live in safer neighborhoods with access to well-maintained community areas and public spaces.

Social inequality is one of the major challenges faced by humanity, which can be seen in various aspects of daily life. One of the main differences between rich and poor people is access to the social environment. People in poverty often live in high-crime and violent areas with little access to safe and community public spaces, which directly affects their quality of life and well-being. In contrast, wealthy people have the ability to live in safer neighborhoods with access to well-maintained community areas and public spaces.

Violence and crime are problems that affect a large portion of the world's population, but especially those in poverty. Often, these individuals live in peripheral areas of big cities where violence is more frequent. These regions typically lack adequate policing and suffer from a lack of basic infrastructure, such as public lighting, sanitation, and transportation services. Additionally, the lack of safe and well-maintained public spaces can harm sociability, leading to isolation and the development of antisocial behaviors.

On the other hand, the wealthy have the opportunity to live in safer neighborhoods with access to community areas and well-maintained public spaces. These areas are important for promoting sociability, social integration, and the building of friendship and solidarity bonds. Furthermore, these areas offer various options for leisure and entertainment, contributing to people's well-being and quality of life.

It is essential to note that access to the social environment is not just a matter of security and leisure but can also influence education, health, and personal development. People in poverty often do not have access to adequate educational spaces, such as libraries and cultural centers, limiting their cognitive and intellectual development. Additionally, the lack of access to adequate health services can lead to illnesses and worsening of medical conditions, reducing the quality and life expectancy.

In contrast, the wealthy have greater access to high-quality health services and more options for choice. This allows for early diagnosis and treatment of diseases and the ability to perform preventive exams, such as regular check-ups. Additionally, these individuals have access to leisure activities, such as clubs, gyms, theaters, and museums, contributing to personal development, cultural improvement, and an increase in quality of life.

The social environment is one of the most important factors that influence people's quality of life, especially those in poverty. The lack of safe public spaces, leisure, and adequate educational options can limit cognitive and intellectual development, as well as reduce quality and life expectancy. Therefore, it is necessary to invest in public policies that promote social quality.

5. Life perspective: People in poverty often face a limited future perspective, with few opportunities for growth and personal development. Wealthy people, on the other hand, often have access to a wide range of opportunities and may have broader and more positive life perspectives.

Life perspective is one of the main differences between people in poverty and the wealthy. While the former often face a limited life with few opportunities for growth and personal development, the latter may have a wide range of opportunities and positive perspectives. This disparity in life perspective has deep roots and is influenced by several factors, including income, education, social environment, and employment opportunities.

People in poverty often face significant obstacles on their journey to improve their life perspectives. The lack of financial resources and limited access to services such as education and health makes it difficult for them to acquire the skills and knowledge necessary to achieve their goals. Additionally, they often face discrimination and prejudice based on their social class, which can lead to demotivation and frustration.

On the other hand, the wealthy have the advantage of financial resources and access to a wide range of opportunities. They often have access to quality education and employment opportunities in fields that offer higher salaries and greater opportunities for growth. Furthermore, they may have access to networking resources that connect them to other influential and successful individuals, allowing them to expand their network and potentially open doors to new opportunities.

However, life perspective is not solely determined by income or access to resources. The social environment also plays a significant role. People in poverty often live in high-crime and violent areas with little access to safe and communal public spaces. This can make it difficult for them to imagine a positive future and develop the necessary confidence to take risks and explore new opportunities.

On the other hand, wealthy people often live in safer neighborhoods with access to well-maintained communal areas and public spaces. This can provide a sense of security and stability that helps build the confidence and motivation necessary to pursue ambitious goals. Additionally, they often have access to quality healthcare services, which allows them to maintain good health and quality of life, improving their future outlook.

The disparity in life perspective between people in poverty and wealthy people is a complex and multifaceted issue. While income and access to financial resources and education play a significant role, the social environment and employment opportunities also play a crucial role. To improve the life perspective of people in poverty, it is important to ensure equal access to quality services, employment opportunities, and a safe and supportive social environment. Additionally, we should work to reduce discrimination based on social class and promote equity in all areas of society.

Chapter 3

Saving Money - The Foundation of Wealth

There is a well-known case in the media about a poor child who became a millionaire by saving money from a very young age. His name is Warren Buffett, one of the richest men in the world and considered one of the greatest investors of all time.

Warren Buffett was born in 1930 in Omaha, Nebraska, United States. His father, Howard Buffett, owned a small brokerage firm, and Warren showed an interest in the business world from a very young age. At the age of 6, he was already selling chewing gum and Coca-Cola bottles to his neighbors, and at the age of 11, he bought his first stocks, using the money he had saved from his job at a local newspaper.

Since then, Buffett has never stopped investing and saving money. He studied economics at the University of Nebraska and then earned a master's degree in economics from Columbia University in New York. In 1956, at the age of 26, he founded his own investment company, Buffett Partnership Ltd.

Buffett became known for his investment style, which is based on buying stocks in solid and secure companies with good long-term growth potential. He is famous for investing in companies like Coca-Cola, American Express, and Gillette, which have become great successes.

Today, at the age of 91, Warren Buffett is one of the richest men in the world, with an estimated fortune of over $100 billion. He is the CEO of Berkshire Hathaway, a holding company that controls over 60 companies in various sectors, such as insurance, retail, energy, and transportation.

Warren Buffett's story is inspiring and shows that, even coming from a poor family, it is possible to achieve financial success through discipline, hard work, and wisdom in investments. The lesson that can be learned from his story is that it is important to save and invest from a young age, as this can bring great rewards in the future.

It is necessary to draw inspiration from great examples like Warren Buffett, and in addition, it is important to plan.

Create a budget: one of the most effective ways to save money is to control your spending and create a budget. It is important to know exactly how much money is coming in and going out of your finances. By creating a budget, you can see where your money is being spent and identify areas where cuts can be made. This allows you to direct more money towards savings and investments.

Managing personal finances is an essential task for achieving financial stability and, consequently, a more prosperous life. Creating a budget is one of the most effective ways to control spending and save money. Below, we present some tips for creating an efficient budget.

The first step is to list all of your fixed and variable expenses, including monthly bills such as rent, water, electricity, phone, and internet, as well as expenses for food, transportation, health, and leisure. It is important to write down everything, even small expenses such as a breakfast at the bakery or a snack on the street. Once you have a clear view of your expenses, it's time to evaluate your spending. Identify areas where you can reduce spending, such as cutting cable TV or opting for a more economical phone plan. This will allow you to save money and direct resources to other areas, such as investments or debt repayment.

Another important tip is to establish priorities. Make sure that essential expenses, such as electricity and water bills, are paid first. Then, set aside a budget for fixed and variable expenses according to your income. Finally, set a goal for savings and invest in actions that help achieve that goal.

When creating a budget, it is important to keep it up-to-date. Review your expenses monthly and make necessary adjustments. This will help you keep track of your finances and save more money over time.

In addition, it is important to set aside a monthly amount for an emergency fund. This is crucial to avoid unnecessary debt in case of unexpected events such as illness, accidents, or unforeseen expenses.

Once you have established a budget, it is important to follow it rigorously. Avoid impulsive spending and stay true to your long-term financial goals. If you encounter difficulties in following the budget, try to identify the reasons and make necessary adjustments.

Finally, it is important to remember that discipline is essential to achieve financial stability and wealth. It is not enough to simply create a budget; you must be consistent and committed to following the saving strategy. With time, patience, and discipline, it is possible to build a solid foundation for wealth and financial prosperity.

1. Save regularly: it is important to save money regularly, even if it is a small amount. By doing so, you are creating a habit of economy and over time, you may see your money grow. Consider creating an emergency fund to deal with unexpected expenses and use a high-interest savings account to maximize your earnings.

Saving money is a fundamental skill for those who wish to have a solid financial foundation and achieve their long-term goals. It is important to keep in mind that saving money does not mean living frugally or depriving oneself of personal pleasures, but rather being conscious and controlling spending. Saving regularly is one of the most important principles for building wealth, as it allows you to accumulate money over time and achieve your financial goals.

One of the first steps to start saving money is to create a detailed budget. This means understanding your regular expenses, such as rent, food, bills, and transportation, as well as additional expenses like entertainment, travel, and hobbies. By having a complete view of your finances, you can identify areas where you can reduce expenses and free up more money to save and invest.

Once you have created a budget, it is important to set realistic and achievable financial goals. Whether it is saving for a trip, buying a house, or making a long-term investment, having a clear goal will help motivate you to save regularly and keep your spending under control. When setting financial goals, it is important to remember that they should be realistic and achievable, taking into account your income and regular expenses.

Another important principle for saving money is to do it regularly, even if it is a small amount. By having a consistent savings routine, you are creating a positive financial habit that can help you achieve your long-term financial goals. To start, consider setting a specific amount that you want to save each month or week and establish a plan to reach that goal.

In addition to saving regularly, it is important to have a strategy for maximizing your earnings. This may include creating an emergency fund to deal with unexpected expenses and using a high-interest savings account to maximize your earnings. When choosing a savings account, it is important to consider the interest rates offered as well as any fees associated with the account.

Finally, it is important to remember that saving money does not have to be a solitary task. Involve your family and friends in your financial goals and establish a support network that can help you achieve your goals. Consider joining savings groups or online communities that share tips and tricks for saving money and investing wisely.

Creating a detailed budget, setting realistic financial goals, saving regularly, maximizing your earnings, and involving your support network are five distinct principles for saving money and building a strong financial foundation. Regular saving is the key to achieving your long-term financial goals and ensuring financial stability. With the right strategy and a little discipline, it is possible to build a healthy financial life.

Saving money is a fundamental strategy for building a wealth base. It is important to keep in mind that while saving money may be challenging, the long-term benefits are significant. One of the most effective ways to achieve this goal is through regular savings. By saving money regularly, you are establishing a healthy financial habit. This means that over time, you will have the ability to save more and more money. To start, begin by saving a small amount of money each week or month. By doing so, you will be creating an emergency fund to handle unexpected expenses.

An emergency fund is an account that you keep reserved for financial emergencies. This account should be easily accessible, but should not be used for daily expenses. Having an emergency fund can help you avoid debt and maintain your finances healthy in times of crisis.

In addition to creating an emergency fund, you should also consider opening a high-interest savings account. High-interest savings accounts pay higher interest rates than regular bank accounts. This means that the more money you deposit in this account, the more money you will earn in interest.

Creating a budget is another fundamental strategy for saving money. Controlling your expenses is essential to keep your finances healthy. When creating a budget, you should list all your monthly expenses and income. This includes fixed bills such as rent or mortgage, utilities, transportation, and food. You should also include variable expenses such as entertainment and clothing.

When creating a budget, it's important to prioritize your expenses. Fixed expenses like housing should be your main priority. After that, you can determine how much money should be allocated for variable expenses like entertainment and clothing. If possible, you should try to reduce your variable expenses. This can include cooking more at home, canceling subscription services you don't use, or buying used clothes.

When saving money, it's important to have clear financial goals in mind. This can include buying a house, a new car, or paying off debt. By setting financial goals, you'll have a specific target to work towards. This can help you stay focused on your financial objectives and resist the temptation to spend money on unnecessary things.

Finally, you should consider investing your money. While saving is an important part of building wealth, it's not enough on its own. Investing your money in stocks, bonds, or real estate can help you increase your wealth in the long run. However, it's important to keep in mind that investing involves risks. Make sure to carefully research your investment options and understand the risks.

Savings is a way of keeping money in a bank account, which offers security and convenience for people who want to save. In savings accounts, deposited money is available to the account holder to be used at any time, without the need for a waiting period. Additionally, savings accounts do not have maintenance fees and offer low but steady profitability.

On the other hand, high-interest savings is a more profitable option for those who want to save money. In this investment modality, banks offer higher interest rates, which means that the invested money earns more. However, in some cases, there may be a waiting period and maintenance fees.

There are several high-interest savings options on the market, such as Tesouro Direto, which allows investors to invest in Brazilian government public bonds, such as Tesouro Selic, which yields according to the country's basic interest rate. Another option is investment funds, which enable investors to invest in various modalities, such as stocks, bonds, real estate, and other options available in the financial market.

Additionally, there are digital bank accounts that offer high-interest savings options without the need to visit a physical branch. These digital accounts also typically offer lower or even free maintenance fees, which reduces costs for the investor.

An example of a high-interest savings option is the Certificado de Depósito Bancário (CDB), which is an investment modality in which the investor lends money to the bank and receives an interest rate in return. The CDB can have different investment periods and interest rates, depending on the issuing bank and the chosen modality.

Another option is the Letras de Crédito Imobiliário (LCI) and Letras de Crédito do Agronegócio (LCA), which are fixed-income securities issued by banks and are tax-exempt for individuals. The LCI and LCA are backed by real estate and agribusiness financing, respectively, and offer more attractive interest rates compared to traditional savings.

Savings is a safe and simple way to keep money, but with low profitability. High-interest savings, on the other hand, offers higher profitability but may have a waiting period and maintenance fees. It's important to evaluate the options available in the market and choose the one that best suits your needs and financial objectives.

2. Avoid Consumer Debt: Consumer debt, such as credit cards and personal loans, can be very expensive and make saving difficult. It is important to avoid these debts whenever possible and seek help to reduce or eliminate existing debt if necessary.

Consumer debt is created to finance the purchase of goods and services that are not considered investments, meaning things that do not generate financial return. The most common types of consumer debt are credit cards, personal loans, and car and home financing.

The problem with consumer debt is that they often have high interest rates, which means that over time, you can end up paying much more for the item than it actually costs. In addition, these debts can make saving difficult and harm your long-term financial health.

Therefore, it is important to avoid consumer debt whenever

possible. The best way to do this is to create a budget and plan your expenses in advance. By doing so, you can identify areas where you can cut expenses and save money. If you need a loan to deal with unexpected expenses, consider low-interest loan options such as secured loans.

If you already have consumer debt, it is important to work to reduce or eliminate it. A good strategy is to pay off the debts with the highest interest rates first while making minimum payments on other debts. This can help reduce costs over time.

Another option is to seek professional help to manage your debts. There are financial advisors who can help you create a plan to deal with your consumer debts and reduce your costs.

A common example of consumer debt is a credit card. Credit cards often have high interest rates, and many people end up accumulating credit card debt due to overspending or a lack of financial planning. If you have a credit card with accumulated debt, it is important to pay more than the minimum payment each month and work to reduce the debt.

Another example of consumer debt is a personal loan. Personal loans are often used to finance larger purchases, such as a car or a trip. However, these loans often have higher interest rates than other types of loans, which means you may end up paying much more for the item than the original price. If you need a personal loan, be sure to compare interest rates and choose the option with the lowest rates.

Finally, car or home financing is another common example of consumer debt. Financing often has lower interest rates than personal loans or credit cards, but can still be expensive over time. It is important to research different financing options and choose one with the lowest interest rates and most favorable terms. It is also important to work to pay off the financing as quickly as possible to avoid the snowball effect.

Consumer debt can be a financial trap for many people, especially those who have little control over their spending. These debts include credit cards, personal loans, car financing, and other forms of credit that are used to finance the purchase of nonessential goods and services or those that cannot be paid with available cash. These debts can be very expensive due to high interest and fees, making saving difficult and leading to default.

To avoid consumer debt, it's important to have a solid financial plan that includes a budget, regular savings, and an emergency fund. This will allow you to control your spending and save money for necessary expenses, avoiding the need to rely on credit to cover these costs. If you already have consumer debt, here are some ways to reduce or eliminate it:

1. Prioritize your debts: If you have multiple consumer debts, start by prioritizing the ones with the highest interest rates. Pay as much as you can towards each one to reduce the balance more quickly and save money on interest over time. Once one debt is paid off, use the money you were paying towards it to pay the next debt with the highest interest rate.

2. Make extra payments: If you can't afford to pay more than the minimum payment on your consumer debts, try making extra payments whenever possible. Even an extra payment of $50 per month can help reduce the balance more quickly and save money on interest over time.

3. Negotiate with creditors: If you're having trouble making payments on your consumer debts, contact your creditors to discuss your options. They may be willing to reduce your interest rates or allow a payment plan with smaller installments and longer terms.

4. Avoid acquiring more debt: While you're trying to reduce your existing consumer debts, it's important to avoid acquiring more debt. Avoid unnecessary purchases and use available cash to pay bills.

5. Consider financial counseling: If you're having trouble managing your consumer debts, consider seeking help from a professional financial counselor. They can help you create a plan to reduce your debts and manage your finances more effectively.

In addition to avoiding consumer debt, it's important to have a solid financial plan that includes regular savings and an emergency fund. This will allow you to be prepared for unexpected expenses and reduce the need to rely on credit to cover them.

Consumer debts, such as credit cards and personal loans, may seem like a quick solution for acquiring desired goods and services. However, these debts can be very expensive and accumulate quickly, leading to serious financial problems. Therefore, it's important to avoid these debts whenever possible and take steps to reduce or eliminate existing debt.

One of the main reasons why consumer debts can be so expensive is due to high interest rates. Credit cards, for example, often have very high interest rates, usually above 20% per year. This means that if you have a balance on your credit card, you'll be paying a significant amount in interest each month, making it difficult to reduce the debt.

Personal loans can also have high interest rates, especially if you have a poor credit history. Interest rates can range from 10% to 30% or more, depending on the lender and your financial situation. This can make the debt even more difficult to pay off and increase your risk of default.

To avoid consumer debt, the best strategy is to spend within your financial means and save up for larger purchases. This may involve creating a budget, setting realistic financial goals, and being disciplined about spending.

If you already have consumer debt, there are several measures you can take to reduce or eliminate the debt. The first step is to assess your financial situation and understand exactly how much you owe and at what interest rate. From there, you can start developing an action plan to pay off the debt.

A common strategy is to make larger payments on your consumer debt with the highest interest rate. This can help reduce the debt more quickly and save money on interest over time. Another option is to consolidate your debts into a lower interest rate loan, which can help simplify your payments and make them more manageable.

It is also important to consider financial counseling if you are struggling with consumer debt. A financial counselor can help you develop a debt repayment plan, provide guidance on how to manage your finances, and help you avoid future consumer debt.

In addition to avoiding consumer debt, another way to improve your finances is to build a good credit score. A strong credit score can help you get loans and credit cards with lower interest rates, which can save you money in the long run.

To build a good credit score, it is important to make payments on time and maintain a low credit card balance.

Consumer debt can be a major obstacle for those looking to establish a solid foundation of personal finances. When it comes to consumer debt, credit cards and personal loans are two of the main culprits. These types of debt can be extremely expensive and difficult to pay off, especially if there is no strategic plan to reduce them.

One of the main reasons consumer debt is so problematic is that it tends to have high interest rates. For example, many credit cards charge annual interest rates of 20% or more. This means that if you have a $5,000 debt on a credit card with a 20% interest rate, you will pay $1,000 in interest each year, or about $83 per month. Personal loans can also have very high interest rates, especially if you do not have a good credit history.

Additionally, consumer debt can make saving difficult. When you are paying a large amount of interest each month, it is harder to save money. This means that you will have less money to invest in your retirement, emergency savings, or other important financial goals.

Fortunately, there are several strategies you can use to avoid consumer debt and reduce or eliminate existing debts. One of the first things you can do is establish a budget and monitor your spending closely. This will allow you to see exactly where your money is going and identify areas where there may be cuts.

Additionally, it is important to be selective about the credit cards you use and limit your purchases to items that you can truly afford. Avoid the temptation to buy things you do not need just because they are on sale or because you want to impress other people.

If you are already in debt, the first thing you should do is contact your creditors and explain your situation. Often, they will be willing to work with you to establish a payment plan that is affordable. You may also consider debt consolidation, which involves getting a loan to pay off your existing debts. This can reduce the interest rates you are paying and make it easier to pay off your debt over time.

Another option is to seek the help of a financial counseling company. These organizations can help you develop a payment plan and provide guidance and support to help you reduce or eliminate your debt. It is important to remember that these services often come with a cost, and it is important to find a reputable company that offers quality services.

Investing in assets is one of the best ways to build long-term wealth. Assets include stocks, real estate, bonds, and other investments that have the potential to generate income or appreciate in value over time. By investing in high-quality assets with potential for appreciation, you can see your investments grow over time.

Assets are defined as anything that can generate income or appreciate in value over time. There are various types of assets available, such as stocks, real estate, bonds, and mutual funds, each with its own advantages and disadvantages.

When investing in assets, it is important to consider your financial goals, risk tolerance, and time horizon. It is always advisable to seek the advice of a financial advisor before investing any money.

Stocks are a common form of asset investment. When you purchase stocks in a company, you become a shareholder and can profit from the company's growth and success. Stocks are traded on stock exchanges, such as the B3 in Brazil, and their prices can fluctuate over time based on economic, political, and market factors. Stocks represent an ownership stake in a company. When you buy stocks, you are investing in the future of the company and the possibility that it will grow and prosper, which can lead to an increase in the value of the stocks you hold. However, it is important to note that stocks can also lose value, and investing in stocks can be risky. It is important to do careful research before investing in a specific company and to diversify your investments across different sectors and companies to minimize risk.

One advantage of investing in stocks is that they offer significantly higher potential returns than other types of investments. However, stock investment is also considered a high-risk investment, as the value of stocks can fall significantly and even become worthless. Therefore, it is important to diversify your stock portfolio to minimize risk.

Real estate is another popular type of asset investment. When you invest in real estate, you buy a property with the goal of profiting from its appreciation and/or rental income. Property appreciation can occur naturally as demand for properties increases or through improvements and renovations to the property.

Real estate offers a more stable potential return than stocks, as properties tend to hold their value over time and also offer rental income. However, investing in real estate can also be considered high-risk, as the real estate market can fluctuate significantly, and expenses related to maintenance, taxes, and insurance can be high. Real estate investment can include buying a property for rental income or participating in real estate funds. Buying properties for rental income can generate passive income and, if the property appreciates over time, can also generate a significant return on investment. Real estate funds allow you to invest in a diversified portfolio of properties, typically with less risk than direct property purchases.

Titles are another option for investing in assets. When you buy a bond, you are lending money to a company or government in exchange for interest. Bonds can be issued by companies, governments, or municipalities, and their interest rates vary based on the credit quality of the issuer and the bond's term. Bonds represent a debt issued by a company or government, with a promise of future payment of interest and principal. By buying bonds, you are lending money to the entity in question and receiving interest in return. Bonds can be a low-risk investment option, but they typically have a lower return than other forms of asset investment. Bonds are considered a low-risk investment because they offer a stable and guaranteed income stream. However, they usually offer a lower return than stocks or real estate.

Mutual funds are another popular form of asset investment. A mutual fund is a type of collective investment that pools money from various investors to purchase a variety of assets, such as stocks, bonds, and other financial instruments. The goal is to achieve a better return than the market average.

Mutual funds are an attractive option for beginner investors or those who do not have the necessary time or knowledge to follow the market.

Other types of asset investments include commodities, such as gold and oil, and alternative investments, such as art investment, fine wines, or rare coins. These types of investments can be riskier than investing in stocks or real estate, but they also have the potential to generate significant returns if you make the right choices.

In addition to investing in assets, it is important to have a long-term investment strategy. Investing in quality assets with long-term appreciation potential can help you achieve your financial goals and provide financial security for the future.

It is also important to have a balanced approach to asset investment. Investing all your money in a single stock or asset type can be too risky. Instead, it is important to diversify your investments in different sectors.

Seek financial education: many people lack basic financial knowledge, which can harm their finances in the long run. Seek financial education to learn how to better manage your finances, invest wisely, and create a long-term plan for wealth. This can involve reading books, participating in seminars and workshops, and consulting a financial professional.

Seeking financial education is essential to ensure a healthier and more stable financial life. Unfortunately, many people have little knowledge about personal finance and, consequently, face financial difficulties throughout their lives. In this context, seeking basic financial knowledge is fundamental so that it is possible to better manage personal finances, invest wisely, and create a long-term plan for wealth.

Financial education is a topic that is not yet widely taught in schools and universities, which often results in people who, although successful in other areas, have little knowledge about financial management. For this reason, seeking information about personal finances should be done proactively. This can involve reading books, participating in seminars and workshops, and consulting a financial professional.

One of the most effective ways to seek financial education is through reading books. There are many books available that address various aspects of personal finance, from budgeting and expense control to investments and long-term financial planning. Some popular books on the topic include "Rich Dad, Poor Dad" by Robert Kiyosaki, "The Richest Man in Babylon" by George S. Clason, and "Secrets of the Millionaire Mind" by T. Harv Eker. Additionally, attending seminars and workshops can be an excellent way to seek financial education. These events are usually conducted by financial experts and can offer an opportunity for interactive learning, as well as the possibility of asking questions and obtaining personalized guidance. Often, these events are held in local communities and can be accessible to a broad audience.

Finally, consulting a finance professional can be a valuable way to seek financial education. A financial advisor can offer personalized guidance based on individual needs, as well as help create a long-term plan for wealth. It is important to remember that not all finance professionals are equal, and it is essential to choose someone who is licensed, experienced, and trustworthy.

In addition to seeking financial education, it is important to develop healthy financial habits. This may include creating a budget, saving regularly, and investing in quality assets. It is also important to avoid consumer debt and cut unnecessary expenses. By developing these healthy financial habits, it is possible to build a solid foundation for long-term wealth.

One of the first steps to seeking financial education is to understand the differences between saving and investing. Saving involves putting money aside for future use, while investing involves putting money into assets with potential for appreciation. Saving is important for creating an emergency fund to deal with unexpected expenses, while investing is important for increasing wealth.

Chapter 4

Cutting Unnecessary Expenses

A famous story about cutting unnecessary expenses is that of Warren Buffett. He is known for his frugality and for living a simple life, despite having a fortune of billions of dollars.

In 2007, Buffett decided to sell his house in Laguna Beach, California, for $4 million. He had bought it in 1971 for $150,000, but decided to sell it because he felt he no longer needed it. Instead, he chose to invest the money in Berkshire Hathaway stocks, his investment company.

Buffett is also known for driving modest cars and not having a private jet, despite his wealth. He prefers to fly on commercial flights and has stated that a private jet is a waste of money.

Additionally, Buffett is famous for his simple and cheap diet. He mainly eats fast food, such as McDonald's burgers, and drinks Coca-Cola daily. He believes that by not spending much money on food, he can invest more in his companies and get bigger returns.

Buffett's example shows that cutting unnecessary expenses is an important part of achieving wealth. By avoiding excessive spending and investing the saved money, it is possible to build a fortune over time.

Cutting unnecessary expenses is one of the best ways to save money and achieve financial independence. When it comes to personal finances, the idea of saving may seem daunting, but the truth is that small changes in our daily habits can make a big difference in our overall budget. There are various ways to cut unnecessary expenses. One of the first things we can do is evaluate our expenses and identify areas where we can save.

This may include reducing entertainment expenses, such as going out to bars and restaurants, or even changing our eating habits, such as opting for home-cooked meals instead of buying ready-made food. Additionally, it's important to think about things we don't use frequently, such as magazine subscriptions or mobile apps, and cancel those expenses.

Another way to cut unnecessary expenses is to change our consumption habits. For example, we can choose to buy clothes from thrift stores instead of spending a fortune on designer pieces. We can also consider swapping the car for cheaper means of transportation, such as bikes or public transport. Additionally, it's important to research and compare prices before buying any item, to ensure we're getting the best possible deal.

One of the biggest expenses that we often overlook is utilities bills, such as electricity, water, and gas. It's possible to save money by reducing energy consumption at home, turning off electronic devices when not in use, taking shorter showers, and installing water-saving devices.

It's also important to evaluate our expenses on banking services, such as checking account fees and credit cards. Sometimes, we may be paying unnecessary fees without realizing it. It's important to compare bank fees and choose an institution that offers the best account options for our needs.

Additionally, we can cut unnecessary expenses by avoiding impulse purchases. It's easy to get carried away by promotions and discounts, but often end up buying things we don't need. It's important to think carefully before making a purchase and evaluate whether we really need the item in question.

Another way to cut unnecessary expenses is to reduce the use of paid services, such as cable TV and streaming services. Often, we don't use all the available channels and programs, and this can end up being a waste of money. By reducing the number of paid services we use, we can save a significant amount of money each month.

Finally, it's important to remember that cutting unnecessary expenses doesn't mean we have to give up all the things we love. We can still have fun and enjoy life, but we need to be aware of our expenses and find ways to save money in areas where we can.

Cutting unnecessary expenses is one of the most effective ways to save money and achieve financial stability. Often, we spend money on things we don't need or that aren't really important to us. By identifying these expenses and eliminating them, we can save money and direct it towards things we truly value.

The first step to cutting unnecessary expenses is to carefully analyze your monthly spending. Make a list of all your expenses, including rent, utilities bills, grocery shopping, and other regular expenses. Then, identify expenses that you can cut or reduce.

For example, you may consider cutting cable TV subscriptions, streaming services, or magazine subscriptions that you don't read. Often, these services are sold as essential, but the truth is that they can be easily replaced with cheaper or even free options. For example, you can consider watching free TV shows online or subscribing to a local library to access magazines and newspapers.

Another way to cut unnecessary expenses is to reduce your food expenses. Often, we spend a lot of money on restaurants and convenience purchases, when we could save money by cooking at home. Consider planning your meals in advance, buying in bulk, and cooking in large quantities to save time and money.

Another way to reduce expenses is to cut back on transportation costs. If you live in a city, consider biking or using public transportation instead of driving or taking a taxi. This can save you a lot of money on gas and parking fees, as well as being healthier and more sustainable.

Another area that can often be trimmed is fashion and beauty. We often spend a lot of money on clothes, shoes, and accessories that we don't need. Consider limiting your fashion purchases to essential pieces and investing in high-quality clothes that will last longer. Additionally, consider buying cheaper beauty products or even making your own products at home using natural ingredients.

Finally, consider cutting expenses related to hobbies and entertainment. We often spend a lot of money on activities that can be replaced by cheaper options. For example, instead of going to expensive bars, consider hanging out with friends for outdoor activities or free events in the city.

Cutting unnecessary expenses can be an effective way to save money and achieve financial stability. By carefully analyzing your spending and identifying expenses that you can cut or reduce, you can save money and direct it towards things that you truly value. Remember that saving is a habit that can be cultivated and developed over time, and that small changes can make a big difference in your financial health.

Cutting unnecessary expenses is one of the most effective ways to save money and increase your ability to save. To get started, it is important to identify which expenses are unnecessary and cut them. Here are some tips to help you do this:

1. Evaluate your expenses

The first step to cutting unnecessary expenses is to understand your finances. Make a list of all your expenses and see where you can cut. Identify which are your fixed expenses, such as rent, car payments, utility bills, insurance, and taxes, and which are your variable expenses, such as food, entertainment, clothing, and accessories. Evaluate each of these expenses and see where you can cut or save.

2. Eliminate frivolous spending

After evaluating your expenses, it's time to eliminate frivolous spending. This may include magazine or newspaper subscriptions that you don't read, cable TV channels that you don't watch, gym clubs that you don't attend, and apps that you don't use. Canceling these subscriptions can free up money that you can use to pay off debts or invest in your savings.

3. Cut back on food expenses

Food is one of the biggest variable expenses that people have. To reduce these expenses, try cooking at home instead of eating out. Buying food on sale and in bulk can also help reduce food expenses. Additionally, reduce consumption of processed and packaged foods, which tend to be more expensive and less healthy.

4. Reduce electricity consumption

Electricity is one of the biggest fixed expenses for families. To reduce this expense, start by turning off electronic devices when not in use, replace incandescent bulbs with LED bulbs, take advantage of natural light, and keep the temperature of the house at a comfortable level but not excessive.

5. Use public or shared transportation

If you don't need to use a car on a daily basis, consider using public or shared transportation, such as bikes or electric scooters. In addition to saving money on fuel, maintenance, and parking, this option can be more eco-friendly.

6. Shop smartly

Buying smart means comparing prices, waiting for promotions, and only buying what you need. Instead of impulse shopping or shopping at expensive stores, compare prices at different stores, research promotions and discount coupons, and shop with a predetermined budget.

7. Avoid consumer debt

Consumer debt, such as credit cards and personal loans, can be very expensive and harm your ability to save. If you have consumer debt, make a plan to eliminate it.

Chapter 5

Developing Habits that Lead to Wealth

Dave Ramsey is an American author, speaker, and radio host who became famous for his financial advice and for helping people get out of debt and achieve financial independence.

In the 1980s, Ramsey had a real estate empire worth millions of dollars. However, he eventually declared bankruptcy due to excessive debts. It was a difficult time for him and his family, but he used this experience to change his financial habits and teach others how to avoid falling into the same situation.

Ramsey created a seven-step plan to get out of debt and achieve financial independence. One of the key steps of the plan is cutting unnecessary expenses. He encourages people to live within their means and avoid frivolous spending. Ramsey also emphasizes the importance of regularly saving money, investing wisely, and living without debt.

Through his radio program and books, Ramsey has helped millions of people change their financial habits and achieve financial independence. His success is an example of how changing habits can lead to wealth and financial success.

Developing healthy financial habits is one of the most effective ways to build long-term wealth. When you are able to maintain positive financial habits, you can save money, invest wisely, and eventually achieve financial stability and independence.

There are several habits that can lead to wealth. Some of the most important include creating a budget, regular saving, smart investing, and financial education.

One of the first habits you should develop is creating a budget. This involves tracking your expenses and creating a monthly spending plan. By having a clear and realistic budget, you can control your spending and identify areas where you can save money. Additionally, you can prioritize your spending based on your long-term financial goals. It is important to review your budget regularly to ensure you are on track to achieving your financial objectives.

Another important habit is regularly saving money. Even if it's a small amount, saving money every month can have a significant impact on your long-term wealth. One of the best ways to save money is to create an emergency fund. This involves saving a specific amount of money to deal with unexpected expenses, such as emergency home repairs or medical expenses. Having an emergency fund can help you avoid using credit cards or high-interest loans to pay for these expenses.

Investing is also an important habit to develop in order to achieve wealth. There are many investment options available, such as stocks, bonds, mutual funds, and real estate.

However, it is important to understand the risk associated with each type of investment and choose options that fit your risk profile and financial goals. Additionally, it is important to regularly monitor your investments and make adjustments as necessary to ensure that you are on the right path to achieving your financial goals.

Finally, seeking financial education is a crucial habit for achieving wealth. This involves learning about financial topics such as investments, saving, budgeting, and debt management. There are many resources available for learning about finance, including books, online courses, seminars, and professional financial advisors. Learning about finance can help you make more informed financial decisions and develop healthy financial habits. Developing healthy financial habits can be challenging, but it is an important step towards achieving long-term wealth. By creating a realistic budget, saving money regularly, investing wisely, and seeking financial education, you can build a solid financial foundation and achieve financial independence.

Building Relationships with Successful People

One famous account on the topic of building relationships with successful people is that of Andrew Carnegie, one of the richest men in the world in the late 19th and early 20th centuries. Carnegie was born into a poor family in Scotland and emigrated to the United States as a teenager. He started working in a cotton factory and later worked for the telegraph company Western Union.

Carnegie stood out for his intelligence and business skills and eventually founded his own steel company, the Carnegie Steel Corporation. He became one of the wealthiest men in the world and a great philanthropist, dedicating much of his wealth to charitable institutions and public causes.

One of the keys to Carnegie's success was his ability to build relationships with successful people. He recognized that he could not achieve success alone and therefore sought to associate himself with people who could help him reach his goals. He established relationships with influential entrepreneurs, politicians, philanthropists, and intellectuals, many of whom became close friends.

Carnegie also recognized the importance of cultivating long-term relationships and investing time and resources into them. He believed that success in business was not just about having a good idea or product, but also about having the right people by your side. He was known for inviting his friends and business partners to dinner at his mansion in New York, where they would discuss ideas and form new partnerships.

The case of Andrew Carnegie shows that building relationships with successful people can be a powerful strategy for achieving wealth and success. By associating with influential people, it is possible to learn from their experiences and knowledge, obtain mentorship and guidance, and gain access to new business opportunities. However, it is important to remember that these relationships must be cultivated with sincerity and respect, and not just as a means of obtaining personal benefits.

Building relationships with successful people is a valuable strategy for those who wish to achieve their financial goals and build long-term wealth. These individuals can offer valuable insights into their own experiences, as well as resources and contacts that can be helpful for your financial success. However, building relationships with successful people is not something that happens overnight. It is a process that requires time, effort, and dedication. In this topic, we will discuss why building relationships with successful people is important and some ways to do so.

Why is building relationships with successful people important? There are several reasons why building relationships with successful people is important for those who want to build long-term wealth. Some of these reasons include:

- Access to resources and contacts: Successful people often have a wide and influential network of contacts. By building relationships with these people, you can have access to resources and contacts that can be useful for your financial success. For example, they may know potential investors, have access to insider information about investments, or be aware of interesting business opportunities.

- Valuable insights: Successful people often have unique experiences and valuable perspectives on finance and business. By building relationships with these people, you can learn from their experiences and gain valuable insights that can help you make more informed financial decisions.

- Mentorship and guidance: Successful people are often willing to share their knowledge and guidance with those who are starting out. By building relationships with these people, you can have the opportunity to receive valuable mentorship and guidance on how to build long-term wealth.

How to build relationships with successful people?

Now that we know why building relationships with successful people is important, let's discuss some ways to do it:

1. Attend networking events: Networking events are a great way to meet successful people and make valuable contacts. Make sure to attend events that are relevant to your financial interests and goals. Be prepared with business cards and a brief description of your financial objectives.

2. Participate in professional organizations: Participating in professional organizations can be an effective way to build relationships with successful people in your area of interest. These organizations can offer networking opportunities, as well as access to valuable resources and information.

3. Volunteer for causes you believe in: Volunteering for causes you believe in can be a great way to meet successful people who share your interests. These people may be involved in similar activities as you and be willing to help you achieve your financial goals.

4. Join online discussion groups: Online discussion groups can be a great way to meet successful people in your industry or area of interest.

Chapter 7

Investing in Stocks: A Beginner's Guide

Poor child, shining shoes to help his mother, succeeded in stocks through dedication. His name, Luiz Barsi Filho.

Born into a lower-middle-class family in São Paulo, Barsi started working at a brokerage firm at the age of 18 and gradually learned about the financial market.

Even without a formal education in the field, Barsi stood out for his dedication and discipline in stock investments. He created his own investment strategy, based on buying stocks of companies that pay good dividends, and remained faithful to it over the years. With a lot of effort and dedication, Barsi became one of the biggest individual investors in the Brazilian stock market. His investment portfolio includes shares in companies such as Banco do Brasil, Petrobras, Vale, among others, and he has already accumulated a fortune estimated in billions of Brazilian reais.

Barsi's success serves as an inspiration for many Brazilians who seek a way out of poverty and to build wealth through investments. He shows that it is possible to succeed in stock investments even without an academic background in the area, as long as one has dedication, discipline, and a well-defined strategy. Investing in stocks may seem intimidating for beginners, but it is a proven way to build long-term wealth. To start, it is important to understand the basic concepts and follow some simple guidelines. The first thing to understand is that stocks represent ownership in a company. When you buy stocks, you are buying a small part of the company and becoming a shareholder. Shareholders have the potential to profit from the growth of the company and can receive dividends, which are regular payments to shareholders based on the company's profits.

Before investing in stocks, it is important to do your research and understand the company in which you are investing. This includes analyzing its products, competitors, financial performance, and future prospects. Additionally, it is important to consider the value of the stocks relative to the current price, which can be done using metrics such as the price-to-earnings ratio.

Another important guideline for beginners is to diversify your investments. This means not putting all your money in a single stock or sector, but spreading your investments across several different companies and sectors. This helps to reduce risk and protects your investments against significant losses.

One way to diversify your investments is to invest in index funds, which are funds that track the performance of a market index such as the S&P 500. This allows you to invest in several different companies at once, without the need to research and buy individual stocks.

Another important guideline is to have a long-term approach to investing in stocks. The stock market can be volatile and fluctuate over time, but historically has shown positive long-term growth. This means that instead of focusing on daily market fluctuations, it is important to keep a focus on the future and invest consistently over time.

Finally, it is important to remember that investing in stocks involves risks and it is important to be prepared for losses. It is important to have an exit strategy in mind if stocks do not meet your expectations and to be aware of the risks involved in each investment.

Investing in stocks can be an effective way to build long-term wealth, but it is important to follow some basic guidelines. Do your research, diversify your investments, have a long-term approach, and be prepared for the risks involved. Over time, you may see your investments grow and reach your financial goals.

Here are some information and tips to help you get started with investing in stocks:

1. Understand what stocks are: Stocks represent ownership of a company. When you buy stocks of a company, you become a shareholder and own a portion of the company.

2. Research companies: Before investing in stocks, it is important to research and understand the companies in which you are considering investing. Consider the company's history, financial performance, market sector, and competition. Make sure to invest in solid and well-managed companies.

3. To invest in stocks, you will need to open a brokerage account. There are many online brokers available that allow you to buy and sell stocks. Be sure to choose a reliable and reputable brokerage firm.

4. Decide how much to invest: Before investing, determine how much money you are willing to risk. Most experts recommend investing only a small percentage of your net worth in stocks.

5. Diversify your investments: Investing in various companies and different sectors can help minimize risk and maximize profit potential. Consider investing in mutual funds or ETFs (Exchange Traded Funds) for easy and instant diversification.

6. Learn to read price charts: Price charts can help you understand the past performance of a stock and predict its future performance. Learn to read price charts and use them to make informed investment decisions.

7. Be patient: Investing in stocks is a long-term game. Don't expect to get rich overnight. Maintain a long-term perspective and don't let short-term fluctuations affect your investment decisions.

8. Stay informed: Stay up to date on market news and the performance of the companies in which you have

invested. Follow trends and adjust your investments according to market changes.

Investing in stocks can be exciting and profitable, but it can also be risky. Be sure to understand the risks involved and make informed investment decisions. With proper research and a solid investment plan, you can begin building your wealth through stock investments.

Chapter 8

Real Estate Investment: Pros and Cons

As the saying goes, "those who buy land don't go wrong". Since ancient times, this has always been a good business, as long as it's done fairly and honestly.

There's a biblical story about investing in real estate. It's told in 1 Kings 21 and involves King Ahab and a man named Naboth.

Ahab was the king of Israel and was interested in a piece of land belonging to Naboth, which was used to grow grapes. He offered Naboth a sum of money for the land, but Naboth refused the offer, stating that the land had been passed down through his family for generations and he didn't want to part with it.

The king was very frustrated with Naboth's refusal, and his wife, Jezebel, suggested a plan to get the land. She forged letters in Naboth's name, accusing him of blasphemy, and had him stoned to death.

After Naboth's death, Ahab took possession of the land and began cultivating it to produce grapes. However, God sent the prophet Elijah to confront Ahab for his sin and prophesied that Ahab's family would be destroyed because of his injustice.

This story teaches us that we should not seek financial gain at any cost, especially if it involves deceit and injustice. Investing in real estate can be a great way to make money, but it's important to do so ethically and fairly, without harming others.

Analyzing Real Estate Investments

Investing in real estate is a popular option for many investors. However, like any investment, there are pros and cons to consider.
Pros:

1. Appreciation Potential: Real estate tends to appreciate over time, especially if it's located in desirable areas. If you buy property in an up-and-coming neighborhood, it's possible that the property value will increase significantly over the years.

2. Passive Cash Flow: If you rent out the property, it can generate passive cash flow through rent. Depending on the property price, rental value, and maintenance costs, it may be possible to get a significant return on investment.

3. Diversification: Investing in real estate can be a way to diversify your investment portfolio. This can be particularly useful if you've already invested in stocks and bonds and want to reduce your portfolio's risk.

4. Control: Unlike other forms of investment, such as stocks, you have more control over a real estate investment. You can make decisions about maintenance, renting, appreciation, and selling the property.

Cons:

1. High Initial Costs: Real estate investment usually requires a large initial investment, including property payment and initial maintenance costs. This can make it difficult for some investors to enter the real estate market.

2. Vacancy Risk: If you're unable to rent out the property, you may have negative cash flow. This can be particularly problematic if you need to make mortgage payments or regular maintenance.

3. Ongoing Maintenance Costs: Real estate requires regular maintenance, such as repairs, upgrades, and cleaning. These costs can quickly accumulate and can affect the investment's profitability.

4. Illiquid: Real estate investment can be less liquid than

other forms of investment, such as stocks. If you need to sell the property quickly, you may have difficulty finding a buyer willing to pay a fair price.

Investing in real estate can be an attractive option for many investors because of its potential for appreciation, passive cash flow, diversification, and control. However, it's important to remember that there are also disadvantages, including high initial costs, vacancy risk, ongoing maintenance costs, and lower liquidity. As with any investment, it's important to do your research and carefully consider your financial goals before deciding to invest in real estate.

Chapter 9

Starting a Business: Opportunities and Risks

An example of current entrepreneurship is the story of Brian Chesky, co-founder and CEO of Airbnb. In 2007, he and his roommate, Joe Gebbia, were having financial difficulties paying the rent for their apartment in San Francisco. They realized that there was a design conference in the city and all the hotels were fully booked, but there were no available rooms for rent. So, they decided to rent out three inflatable mattresses in their living room and provide breakfast for the guests.

The idea was a success, and soon Chesky and Gebbia decided to create an online platform that connected people who needed accommodation with hosts who had available space. Airbnb was founded in 2008 and started with just a few apartments in San Francisco, but soon expanded to other cities and countries.

Today, Airbnb is valued at over $100 billion and is considered one of the most valuable technology companies in the world. Chesky led the company through various challenges, including the global COVID-19 pandemic, which deeply impacted the travel and hospitality industry. However, he and his team found new ways to innovate and adapt to the changing needs of customers, including virtual experiences and new cleaning and safety features.

The success of Airbnb and Chesky's leadership demonstrate the importance of being attentive to opportunities, being creative, and being willing to take risks. It also highlights the importance of listening to customers and adapting to their constantly changing needs. Chesky and his team are an inspiring example of current entrepreneurship and how innovation can lead to great business success.

Starting a business can be an exciting journey filled with opportunities, but it can also involve significant risks. When considering the possibilities, it's important to weigh the pros and cons to make the right decision. Below are some opportunities and risks to consider when starting a business.

Opportunities:

1. Autonomy: One of the main advantages of owning a business is having total control over your decisions and direction. You are your own boss and can decide how you want to run your business and which direction to take.

2. Flexibility: Having your own business allows for more flexibility regarding work hours and work-life balance. This can be particularly beneficial if you have other responsibilities, such as caring for your family.

3. Profit potential: If the business is successful, the potential for profit can be significant. You have the opportunity to earn more than would be possible in a traditional job.

4. Creativity: Having your own business allows you to be more creative in your marketing approach, product development, and business approaches. This can be particularly rewarding for those with a penchant for innovative thinking.

Risks:

1. Uncertainty: Starting a business can be an uncertain and lengthy process. It's possible that you may not see significant profits for a long period of time, if ever. Uncertainty can be stressful and can involve significant financial risk.

2. Financial liability: Starting a business requires initial

capital, which is often funded by the owner or outside investors. This can lead to significant debts, and the owner is responsible for paying them back, even if the business fails.

3. Competition: It can be challenging to compete with established businesses, especially if they have a loyal customer base. It's important to do your market research and ensure that you have a unique selling proposition that differentiates your business from the competition.

4. Overwork: Owning a business can involve long work hours, especially in the early stages. This can affect your personal life and can lead to an excessive workload that can be difficult to manage.

Starting a business can be an exciting and rewarding experience, but it can also involve significant risks. Before making a decision, it's important to carefully consider the pros and cons, do your research, and carefully plan the start of your business. With proper planning, hard work, and dedication, it's possible to succeed in the business world.

Franchises

An option that has become increasingly popular is investing in franchises. Franchises offer a ready and established business model, with a brand that is already recognized in the market. This reduces some of the risks associated with traditional entrepreneurship, such as lack of experience in the industry and uncertainty about the business's success.

Additionally, franchises usually offer support to franchisees, including training, marketing guidance, and technical assistance.

This can help the entrepreneur feel more secure and increase the chances of success.

Another advantage of franchises is that they have greater bargaining power with suppliers, which can result in lower prices for the products and services offered. This can increase profit margins and make the business more profitable.

However, investing in a franchise also presents some risks and disadvantages. The initial cost of becoming a franchisee can be high, including franchise fees and ongoing royalties. Additionally, the franchisee is usually required to follow the policies and guidelines established by the franchise, which can limit the entrepreneur's creativity and flexibility.

Another risk associated with franchises is brand dependency. If the franchise has a negative image or faces reputation problems, this can directly affect the franchisee's business performance.

Before investing in a franchise, it is important to do careful research on the brand and industry it operates in. The franchisee should evaluate the costs and benefits of the investment, as well as consider whether the franchise aligns with their personal values and goals.

Investing in a franchise can be an exciting and lucrative opportunity for novice entrepreneurs. However, it is important to remember that every investment involves risks and it is essential to do careful research and evaluate the costs and benefits before making a decision.

Angel Investors

Angel investors are high net worth individuals who provide capital to startups or early-stage companies in exchange for an equity stake in the company. They are known as "angels" because they provide financial resources when the company is in its early stage and needs help getting off the ground.

These investors usually have business experience and are able to provide valuable guidance and advice to novice entrepreneurs. They can also help leverage connections and resources that entrepreneurs may not have access to otherwise.

Angel investors can invest in a wide range of sectors and companies, from technology and healthcare to food and retail. They usually invest smaller amounts than venture capitalists and can make investments in earlier stages of the company's development.

One of the main advantages of having an angel investor is that they can provide financial resources and knowledge that can help accelerate the company's growth. Additionally, they can help attract other investors and provide credibility to the company.

However, there are also some risks associated with having an angel investor. They usually have an equity stake in the company and may have expectations about how the company is managed and how resources are used. Additionally, if the company is not successful, the investment can become a significant loss for the angel investor.

To initiate the process of attracting angel investors, entrepreneurs typically need to have a solid business plan and an experienced management team. They should also be prepared to give up a portion of ownership in the company in exchange for the investment.

When seeking angel investors, it's important to find those who have experience in the industry in which the company operates and can provide valuable guidance. Entrepreneurs should also be prepared to negotiate fair terms and conditions with angel investors.

Angel investors typically focus on investing in startups that operate in sectors where they have experience and knowledge, in order to minimize investment risk. They also tend to invest in companies that have a well-crafted business plan and a promising business model.

However, there are some risks associated with investing in startups, especially as many companies fail in their early stages. Additionally, investing in early-stage companies is often illiquid, which means that the invested money may be tied up for a long time before generating returns.

To mitigate these risks, many angel investors choose to invest in a diversified portfolio of early-stage companies rather than putting all their capital into a single company. They may also opt to invest in companies that are in a more advanced stage of development, such as those that already have established revenue or customers. In general, angel investing can be an attractive option for entrepreneurs seeking funding to start or expand their businesses. However, it's important to keep in mind that there are risks associated with this type of investment and that it's crucial to carefully evaluate each opportunity before deciding to invest. Entrepreneurs should be aware of these risks and be prepared to work in partnership with the angel investor to ensure the success of the company.

Chapter 10

Mistakes to Avoid When Investing

One of the most well-known cases of financial mismanagement occurred with the American company Enron, which was considered one of the world's largest energy companies in the 1990s.

Enron was founded in 1985 and, over the years, expanded its businesses to other areas such as communications and financial services. The company grew rapidly and became one of the most valuable companies in the United States.

However, the company concealed financial and accounting problems by creating a complex structure of offshore companies and manipulating its balance sheets to hide losses. In addition, the company's executives engaged in unethical and illegal practices, such as bribery and price manipulation.

In 2001, the truth came to light and Enron went bankrupt, leaving thousands of investors and employees without money. The company's executives were prosecuted and sentenced to years in prison, including Enron's CEO, Jeffrey Skilling.

The Enron case is a clear example of the dangers of irresponsible and corrupt financial management. The company grew rapidly, but this was not sustainable due to the lack of integrity in its business practices. The case also led to changes in corporate governance laws and financial regulation in the United States to prevent similar situations from occurring in the future.

Therefore, it is important for companies and individuals to have responsible and ethical financial management to avoid errors that can lead to serious consequences and impact the lives of many people.

Investing can be an effective way to build long-term wealth, but it can also be a risky and trap-filled activity. To avoid losing money and maximize your returns, it is important to know and avoid the main mistakes made by both novice and experienced investors. On this page, we will discuss some of the most common mistakes to avoid when investing.

1. Not doing your research: Many novice investors fail to do the proper research before investing. They may follow the advice of friends or coworkers without considering the investment's history or the experience of the individuals offering the advice. It is important to research the company or sector in which you plan to invest, evaluate its fundamentals and prospects, and consider the experience of fund managers or financial analysts before making an investment decision.

2. Investing in something you don't understand: Investing in a sector or financial product that you don't understand can be dangerous. It is important to have a solid understanding of the investment in question, the risks involved, and the potential for returns before investing your money. If you are not familiar with a particular sector or financial product, it is best to avoid investing until you have acquired more knowledge and experience.

3. Ignoring diversification: Diversification is one of the most important strategies for minimizing investment risk. Investing in a single stock or sector can be risky because a negative event can significantly affect the value of your investment. It is best to diversify your investments across various sectors and financial products to minimize risk and maximize potential returns.

4. Market timing: Trying to predict the best time to buy or

sell stocks can be very difficult and often leads to losses. Markets are unpredictable and can fluctuate significantly in the short term. It is best to adopt a long-term investment strategy and not worry about short-term market fluctuations. The goal should be to find quality investments and hold them for a longer period of time.

5. Neglecting costs: Investment costs, including brokerage fees, taxes, and other related expenses, can significantly reduce your returns over time. It is important to consider all costs involved when choosing a broker or investment manager and to keep overall investment costs as low as possible.

6. Not having a plan: Many novice investors invest without a clear plan or objective in mind. It is important to have a well-defined investment plan that takes into account your long-term goals, risk tolerance, and investment horizon. The plan should include a diversification strategy and a process for monitoring the performance of your portfolio and making adjustments as necessary.

7. Being overly emotional: Investing is often an emotional activity and can be difficult to remain calm. Many disastrous mistakes are made by making hasty and irrational decisions in moments of pressure and tension, and later regret sets in when analyzing the facts with a calmer mind.

Chapter 11

Acquiring Sources of Passive Income

There are many examples of people who have built a financial empire through passive income sources, but one unusual and interesting case is that of Pat Flynn, a blogger and entrepreneur who stumbled upon an unexpected source of income.

In 2008, Pat was laid off from his job as an architect in the midst of the financial crisis. He decided to start a blog about how to pass the architecture exam and help others succeed in the field. His blog, "The Smart Passive Income Blog," quickly became a success, gaining thousands of followers and generating significant income through advertising and affiliate marketing.

However, the passive income source that Pat discovered was even more unexpected. He decided to create an e-book about how to pass the architecture exam and offered it on his blog for just $19.99. To his surprise, the e-book became a bestseller, selling over 7,000 copies in its first year and generating significant passive income.

Encouraged by his success, Pat continued to create e-books and online courses in various areas, including personal finance, online business, and marketing. He also began investing in real estate and index funds, creating multiple sources of passive income and building a financial empire.

Today, Pat Flynn is one of the leading experts in online entrepreneurship and passive income sources. His blog, podcasts, and books inspire thousands of people around the world to pursue their dreams of building a financially independent life. His success is an inspiring example of how a simple idea and a little effort can lead to significant passive income and even a financial empire.

Acquiring passive income sources is one of the best ways to achieve financial independence. Unlike active income, which is obtained through work, passive income is generated with little or no continuous effort after the initial investment.

There are several ways to acquire passive income sources, and each has its pros and cons. Some of the most popular forms include:

1. Fixed income investments: Investing in bonds, real estate funds, and other fixed income investments can provide a reliable source of passive income. These investments usually offer a fixed interest rate or dividends, allowing you to know exactly how much passive income you will receive each month.

2. Real estate rental: Renting a property, whether it is a house, apartment, or commercial space, can generate significant passive income. However, this requires a considerable initial investment and ongoing property management.

3. Stock dividends: Some companies regularly pay dividends to shareholders, providing a source of passive income. However, this can be volatile and dividends may be reduced or eliminated in times of crisis.

4. Affiliate programs: Participating in affiliate programs, where you earn a commission for every sale you generate through your affiliate link, can be an easy and scalable way to earn passive income. This requires some initial effort to promote the product or service, but after that, it is relatively simple.

5. Intellectual property: If you have creative skills, you can create digital products such as e-books, online courses, music, or software, and sell them online. Once the

product is created and made available for sale, you can earn money without having to do anything else.

However, there are some common mistakes that people make when acquiring passive income sources. Some of these include:

1. Not conducting research: It's important to conduct thorough research before investing in any passive income source. This may include risk analysis, verifying the legitimacy of the opportunity, and evaluating competition.
2. Relying on a single passive income source: It's important to diversify your passive income sources to reduce risk. If you rely on a single passive income source and something goes wrong, you could lose all of your income.
3. Not investing enough time and effort: Even with passive income sources, it's still necessary to invest initial time and effort to build and maintain the income source. Ignoring this can lead to a loss of income.
4. Ignoring compliance: It's important to ensure that your passive income source is in compliance with local tax laws. Ignoring this can lead to fines and penalties.

Acquiring passive income sources can be a great long-term wealth-building strategy. Passive income is a stream of money that is generated without the need for active involvement in the process. This can include investments in dividend-paying stocks, rental income from properties, investments in real estate funds, royalties from intellectual property, and more.

One of the main advantages of acquiring passive income sources is the freedom it provides. Over time, a passive income source can become sufficient to cover your basic expenses, allowing you to have more flexibility in terms of work and lifestyle. Additionally, having multiple passive income sources can help diversify your investment portfolio and reduce financial risk.

However, it's important to be cautious when acquiring passive income sources and avoid get-rich-quick schemes or risky investments. Thorough research and evaluation of the viability and stability of passive income sources before investing is necessary. Additionally, it's important to remember that passive income sources often require an initial investment and time to grow, so patience and financial discipline are necessary for long-term positive results.

Some of the most common ways to acquire passive income sources include:

Dividend-paying stocks: Many companies distribute a portion of their profits to shareholders in the form of dividends, which can be a source of passive income for investors. It's important to research companies carefully before investing to ensure they have a stable and reliable dividend payment history.

- Rental income from properties: Investing in rental properties is one of the most well-known ways to acquire passive income sources. However, it's important to remember that real estate investment can be expensive and requires specific knowledge to be successful. Additionally, property maintenance and tenant relationship management must be considered.

- Real estate fund investments: Real estate funds are a way to invest in properties without having to buy them directly. They function as an investment pool, where investors' money is used to acquire and manage a portfolio of properties. Investors receive a regular income distribution based on the fund's performance.

- Intellectual property investments: Investing in intellectual property, such as patents, trademarks, and copyrights, can be a way to generate passive income. However, it's important to remember that registering and protecting intellectual property can be expensive, and the viability and market demand must be evaluated before investing.

- Affiliate programs: Affiliate programs allow you to promote products or services on your website or social network and earn a commission on sales made.

Chapter 12

Overcoming your limits and taking calculated risks

The story of investor Paul Tudor Jones.

Jones grew up in Memphis, Tennessee, and developed a fascination for financial markets from an early age. He began trading commodity futures while still a college student in the 1970s, and after graduating with a degree in economics, he went to work for brokerage firm E.F. Hutton.

In 1980, at just 26 years old, Jones founded his own investment management company, Tudor Investment Corporation. His investment strategy was based on technical and fundamental analysis, combining different market indicators to make buying and selling decisions.

In the 1980s, Jones stood out for his accurate predictions regarding the foreign exchange market and his skill in managing risks. He was one of the first investors to bet against the British currency during the 1992 currency crisis, known as "Black Wednesday," and made over $1 billion from the operation.

However, the most challenging moment of his career came in 2008, during the global financial crisis. At that time, his company suffered significant losses, and Jones had to take big risks to recover the losses.

He decided to invest in stock index futures contracts, a risky strategy amidst market turbulence. Jones purchased contracts worth $1.1 billion, betting that the market would recover in the following months.

His bet paid off. Starting in March 2009, the market began to recover, and Tudor Investment Corporation recovered its losses in just a few months. Jones became known as one of the few investors who managed to stand out during the global financial crisis.

The story of Paul Tudor Jones is an example of how overcoming limits and taking calculated risks can lead to great achievements in finance. Jones had to face challenges and take risks throughout his career but always knew how to adapt and find new investment opportunities. Today, his fortune is valued at over $6 billion.

Taking calculated risks can be an important step in achieving success in various areas of life, including career and finance. However, this attitude can generate fear and insecurity in many people, who prefer to stay in their comfort zone and avoid any possibility of failure. To overcome your limits and take calculated risks, it is necessary to follow some strategies.

Firstly, it is important to evaluate risks and potential consequences before making a decision. It is necessary to consider various factors, such as financial impact, time and effort involved, possibility of failure, and expected benefits. To make a more accurate assessment, it is recommended to seek information and guidance from experts in the field.

In addition, it is important to be prepared to deal with the consequences of possible failure. This includes having a plan B in case things do not go as planned, and being willing to learn from mistakes and seek new opportunities. It is essential not to give up at the first obstacle, but rather to look for solutions and alternatives to overcome challenges.

Another important strategy is to seek self-awareness and personal development.

By understanding your own abilities, limitations, and values, it's possible to identify opportunities that best suit your profile and create a more effective action plan. Additionally, investing in courses, training, and networking can help expand possibilities and reduce risks involved.

Finally, it's important to remember that taking calculated risks does not mean acting impulsively or without planning. You need to have a clear and strategic vision, well-defined goals, and a detailed action plan. This way, it's possible to maximize the chances of success and minimize the risks involved.

Overcoming your limits and taking calculated risks can be an important step towards achieving success in various areas of life. To do this, it's necessary to assess the risks, be prepared to deal with the consequences, seek self-awareness and personal development, and have a strategic and well-planned vision. With these strategies, it's possible to increase the chances of success and build a more fulfilled and satisfying life.

Chapter 13

Navigating Fear and Limiting Beliefs

One of the most inspiring stories about overcoming fear and limiting beliefs in finance is that of Chris Gardner, an American entrepreneur and investor who became famous for his life story portrayed in the movie "The Pursuit of Happyness".

Chris Gardner went through many financial and personal difficulties. He grew up in a poor family, suffered abuse from his stepfather, and had problems with the law. As an adult, he worked as a medical equipment salesman and, for a period, as a representative of a stock brokerage. However, he never made much money and ended up becoming homeless with his young son.

Despite the difficulties, Gardner never lost faith in himself and his abilities. He had a great passion for the financial market and believed he could become a successful investor. Even without academic training in the field, he studied hard, read books about investments, and learned to analyze the market.

Over time, Gardner managed to make some investments that earned him money, and gradually built his fortune. Today, he is one of the world's biggest investors and founded his own investment firm, Gardner Rich.

Chris Gardner's story shows how it's possible to overcome fears and limiting beliefs and build a prosperous financial life. He didn't let his past difficulties prevent him from taking calculated risks and investing in himself. Instead, he dedicated himself to learning and developing skills that made him successful.

Navigating fear and limiting beliefs is an important skill to achieve success and happiness in any area of life. Often, our limiting beliefs and fears prevent us from making important decisions and taking new risks, keeping us stuck in our comfort zone. However, it's possible to overcome these barriers and take calculated risks to achieve our goals.

To start navigating fear and limiting beliefs, it's important to first identify them. This may involve reflecting on our greatest concerns and fears regarding a particular situation or goal, as well as exploring any negative or limiting thoughts we may have. By identifying these barriers, we can begin to work to overcome them.

One of the best ways to overcome fear and limiting beliefs is through action. Often, fear arises due to uncertainty or lack of experience in a certain area. By taking steps to increase our knowledge and experience, we can reduce fear and feel more confident in our decisions. This may involve conducting research, seeking guidance from a mentor or coach, or participating in relevant trainings or workshops.

Additionally, it is important to develop a growth mindset and be willing to learn from our mistakes. Instead of getting stuck in fear of failure, we should see each failure as an opportunity for learning and growth. This will help us feel more confident and resilient as we take bigger risks.

Another important strategy is to surround ourselves with positive and encouraging people. The influence of friends, family, and colleagues can have a significant impact on our ability to overcome fear and limiting beliefs. By surrounding ourselves with people who support and believe in us, we can feel more confidence and encouragement to take bigger risks and move forward towards our goals.

Finally, it is important to remember that overcoming fear and limiting beliefs does not happen overnight. It requires time, effort, and constant practice. However, by focusing on your goals, developing a growth mindset, and being willing to take calculated risks, you can begin to overcome your personal barriers and achieve the success and happiness you desire.

Chapter 14

The Importance of Personal Development

In 1967, American writer and speaker Jim Rohn met a young man named Tony Robbins. Robbins was going through a tough time in his life, working as a janitor at a school and struggling to make ends meet on a low salary. He wanted to change his life and have more success, but he didn't know where to start.

That's when Robbins discovered Jim Rohn's lectures and decided to invest in his personal development. He started reading books on business, finance, and psychology, and attending lectures from other personal development experts. Robbins worked tirelessly to apply these teachings to his life and career.

After years of hard work and dedication to personal development, Robbins became one of the most renowned and successful speakers in the world, inspiring millions of people to achieve their goals and change their lives. He founded several successful companies, including Robbins Research International, a personal development and training company, and the Life Mastery Institute, a company that helps coaches transform their careers and impact their communities.

However, in 2001, Robbins faced one of the biggest tragedies of his life. His mother, who was suffering from advanced stage cancer, passed away in his arms. He was devastated and had difficulty coping with the loss. In his pain, he realized that there was still much work to be done in his own personal development.

Robbins decided to channel his pain and grief into a greater purpose, helping other people overcome their own adversities and develop the skills needed to achieve success and happiness. He created the Anthony Robbins Foundation, which is dedicated to helping people in crisis situations such as hurricane victims, fire victims, and other emergencies.

Tony Robbins' story is a powerful example of the importance of personal development for success in life. His experiences show that even when facing the worst tragedies, we can use that pain to become stronger, more compassionate, and more successful individuals. It's a reminder that regardless of the circumstances, we can always overcome and achieve our goals if we dedicate ourselves to our own personal growth.

Personal development is an ongoing process of improving skills, knowledge, and values that help people achieve their goals and improve their lives. It's an investment in oneself that leads to personal and professional growth. The importance of personal development is broad and can have positive impacts in all areas of life.

One of the main reasons to invest in personal development is to improve self-confidence and self-esteem. When people feel more confident in their abilities and capabilities, they are more likely to take risks and pursue their goals. Personal development can help overcome limiting beliefs and fears that hinder progress and achieving success.

In addition, personal development can lead to better decision-making. This is because when people have more knowledge and experience, they are able to analyze situations more clearly and choose the best option. This can lead to more positive outcomes in all areas of life, including relationships, career, and finances.

Another advantage of personal development is the improvement of interpersonal communication. By learning to communicate more effectively, people can establish healthier and constructive relationships with coworkers, friends, and family. Effective communication can also help resolve conflicts and avoid misunderstandings.

Personal development can also lead to greater resilience and adaptability. When people have problem-solving skills and mental flexibility, they are better able to deal with change and adversity. This can be especially useful in times of uncertainty, such as during a pandemic or financial crisis.

There are many ways to seek personal development, such as reading self-help books, participating in workshops, courses, and training, coaching, and therapy. It can also be helpful to engage in activities that challenge skills and lead to personal growth, such as learning a new language, practicing a new sport or hobby.

Personal development is essential for achieving success and improving quality of life. Investing in oneself and improving skills, knowledge, and values can lead to greater self-confidence, better decision-making, more effective interpersonal communication, resilience, and adaptability in times of change.

Chapter 15

Creating a Wealth Mindset

Nathalia Arcuri is a famous Brazilian financial educator, creator of the "Me Poupe!" YouTube channel, and author of the book "Me Poupe! - 10 Steps to Never Lack Money in Your Pocket". Her story is an inspiring example of how to create a wealth mindset.

Before becoming a personal finance expert, Nathalia went through many financial difficulties. She had to deal with a series of challenges, including debts, unemployment, and even the loss of her apartment. However, instead of giving up, she decided to take control of her finances and change her life.

Nathalia started by studying everything she could about personal finance. She read books, attended lectures, and took courses to learn everything she could about money and investments. She also began to put into practice the techniques she learned, such as creating a budget and reducing unnecessary expenses.

Over time, Nathalia began to see results. She paid off her debts, created an emergency fund, and started investing in stocks and real estate funds. She also decided to share her experiences and knowledge with others, creating the YouTube channel "Me Poupe!".

Today, Nathalia is one of the biggest influencers in Brazil when it comes to personal finance. Her YouTube channel has more than 6 million subscribers, and she has helped thousands of people change their financial lives. Nathalia believes that the key to creating a wealthy mindset is knowledge and practice. She encourages people to learn as much as they can about personal finance and to put into practice the techniques they learn, even if it's a little bit at a time.

Nathalia's story shows how it's possible to create a wealthy mindset, even in the face of financial difficulties. With dedication, study, and practice, she transformed her life and now helps others do the same.

Creating a wealthy mindset is essential to achieving financial independence and living a prosperous life. This mindset doesn't just mean having money, but also having the ability to create wealth and keep it over time. Developing a wealthy mindset involves changes in the way we think and act about money. Here are some tips for creating a wealthy mindset:

1. Believe in yourself: Self-confidence is crucial to achieving financial success. Believe that you have what it takes to achieve your financial goals, and don't be afraid to take calculated risks to achieve them.

2. Set your financial goals: Set clear and realistic financial goals and create a plan to achieve them. This will help maintain financial focus and discipline, as well as allow you to evaluate your progress over time.

3. Financial education: Invest in your financial education by learning about personal finance, investments, business, and entrepreneurship. Financial knowledge is a powerful tool for creating wealth and avoiding financial mistakes.

4. Practice gratitude: Gratitude is an attitude that helps create a positive mindset. Be thankful for what you have and what you've already achieved, instead of focusing on what's missing. Gratitude can help you feel more fulfilled and attract more prosperity into your life.

5. Eliminate limiting beliefs: Often, our limiting beliefs can prevent us from achieving our financial goals. Identify the beliefs that are preventing your financial success and replace them with positive and motivating thoughts.

6. Be persistent: The path to wealth can be long and challenging. It's important to be persistent and persevere in the face of challenges and obstacles. Stay focused on your goals and keep moving forward, even when things seem difficult.

7. Be grateful: Gratitude is one of the foundations of a wealthy mindset. Be grateful for what you already have and for the good things that are yet to come. Remember that money is just one of the many things that bring happiness and fulfillment.

By creating a wealthy mindset, it's possible to achieve financial goals and live a prosperous life. This mindset involves changes in the way we think and act about money, including self-confidence, financial education, gratitude, and persistence. By developing these characteristics, it's possible to transform your financial life and achieve financial success.

Chapter 16

Recompense: the Importance of Charity and Philanthropy

Bill Gates is one of the greatest philanthropists of our time. The Microsoft co-founder and his wife, Melinda Gates, founded the Bill and Melinda Gates Foundation in 2000, which is now one of the largest and most influential philanthropic foundations in the world. Since then, the Foundation has worked in various areas such as health, education, and global development, donating billions of dollars to social causes.

Gates is known for his philanthropy and commitment to improving the world. In 2010, he and Melinda created "The Giving Pledge," a campaign that calls on billionaires around the world to donate at least half of their fortunes to philanthropic causes during their lifetimes or in their wills. Since then, more than 200 billionaires have joined the campaign, pledging to donate over $500 billion.

The Bill and Melinda Gates Foundation has also been a leading supporter in the fight against the COVID-19 pandemic. Since the beginning of the pandemic, the Foundation has donated billions of dollars for vaccine research and development, as well as providing health assistance and medical supplies to developing countries.

In addition, Gates has been an active advocate for education and opportunities for young people around the world. He believes that education is fundamental to improving people's lives and creating a more equal world. In 2015, he launched "The Gates Millennium Scholars Program," an initiative that offers scholarships to minorities and low-income students so they can attend college.

Bill Gates is an example of one of the greatest philanthropists of our time, committed to helping improve people's lives and creating a more just and equal world. His foundation has supported various important causes, including the fight against the COVID-19 pandemic, and his work has inspired many others to do the same.

Recompense is an important topic that encompasses charity and philanthropy. The idea of giving back to society is one of the noblest and most important that we can adopt in our lives. It is important to understand that, although we often confuse charity with philanthropy, these two practices have their own characteristics and ways of being executed.

Charity is an act of generosity, in which something is donated to help another person. This act can be done by individuals or organizations, and can be material or non-material. Charity can be carried out in various forms, such as donating food, clothing, money, time, and even specific skills. Charity is a way to alleviate the pain and suffering of people who are in vulnerable situations.

Philanthropy, on the other hand, is a more structured and planned act that seeks to impact society on a large scale. It is a systematic and planned action that aims to bring about long-term social change. Philanthropy involves donating resources to specific causes, such as education, health, the environment, among others. The goal of philanthropy is to cause a positive impact on society, not just alleviate a specific situation.

The importance of charity and philanthropy is enormous. By helping those in need, we are making a difference in their lives and contributing to a more just and equal world. Charity and philanthropy also allow us to develop empathy and solidarity, fundamental characteristics for individual and collective well-being.

In addition, practicing charity and philanthropy can also bring benefits to our own lives. Studies show that helping others can increase our sense of happiness and well-being, as well as reduce stress and anxiety.

We can also feel more fulfilled and satisfied with our own lives by knowing that we are making a difference in the lives of others. However, it's important to remember that charity and philanthropy are not the only forms of giving back. We can find ways to contribute to society in our daily lives, such as by respecting the environment, participating in community actions, and volunteering. Every action, no matter how small, can make a difference in someone's life.

Giving back is an important practice that should be incorporated into our lives. Charity and philanthropy are meaningful ways to give back to society, but there are other ways to make a difference. By practicing giving back, we are contributing to a more just and equal world, and also to our own emotional and psychological well-being.

Chapter 17:

Teaching Financial Literacy to Children

In a world where financial education is not highly valued, teaching children how to manage money can be a significant challenge. However, there are people dedicated to this cause, such as John Lanza, an American entrepreneur who founded "The Money Mammals", a company that aims to teach financial literacy to children in a fun and interactive way.

It all started when John realized that many adults didn't know how to handle money, and that this was due to a lack of financial education in childhood. So, he decided to create a solution for this problem and founded "The Money Mammals", a company that offers financial education programs for children of various ages.

The programs include activities, games, and even songs so that children can learn in a playful and fun way. Additionally, the company offers educational books and resources to help parents and educators teach finance effectively.

The idea was so successful that John's company has won several awards and gained recognition in various media outlets. Nowadays, "The Money Mammals" has reached thousands of children in the United States and is expanding to other countries.

John Lanza's work is an inspiring example of how financial education can be transformed into a fun and meaningful experience for children. Teaching children how to handle money from an early age can help them become more financially conscious and responsible adults, which can have a positive impact on their lives and the economy as a whole.

Financial literacy is an essential skill for anyone who wants to manage their personal finances successfully. Teaching this skill to children from an early age is a way to ensure that they have a healthy financial life in the future. But how can we teach financial literacy to children effectively?

One of the simplest ways to start is to teach children the difference between money and value. Money is a currency or note that we use to buy things, while value is the benefit we receive from spending that money. For example, when we buy a toy, we are spending money, but the value is the fun the child will have playing with it. This understanding helps children realize that money is not infinite and that we need to spend it wisely.

Another important concept is budgeting. It is essential to teach children the importance of having a budget and how to create one. We can help them identify their fixed expenses, such as housing, food, and transportation, as well as their variable expenses, such as clothing and entertainment. This way, they can have a clear idea of how much money they have available to spend.

It is also important to teach children about saving and investing. This can be done in a fun way, such as creating a piggy bank to save money or a board game that simulates investments. This way, children learn about the power of saving and how money can grow over time.

Another fundamental aspect is teaching children about debt and credit. They should understand that debt can be a useful tool but can also become a trap if not managed properly. It is important to teach them the importance of not spending more than they earn and to avoid consumer debt, such as credit cards.

Finally, we can encourage children to think about entrepreneurship and business. Many children have creative ideas and can start small businesses at home, such as selling crafts or offering pet care services. This can teach them important lessons about entrepreneurship, financial management, and responsibility.

Teaching financial literacy to children may seem challenging, but it is an essential skill that will help children have a healthy financial life in the future. We can start with simple concepts, such as money, value, and budgeting, and gradually introduce more complex ideas, such as saving, investing, and entrepreneurship. This way, we are investing in the financial future of our children and helping them have a more prosperous and secure future.

Chapter 18

Maintaining Prosperity in the Family

One of the most well-known examples of maintaining prosperity in the family is the story of the Rockefellers. The family, which started out humble, was able to build a financial empire thanks to John D. Rockefeller's success in the Standard Oil Company in the late 19th century.

However, financial success was not the only focus of the Rockefeller family. They also highly valued philanthropy and social responsibility. John D. Rockefeller believed that his wealth should be used to help those in need, and therefore, he and his children generously donated to noble causes such as education and healthcare.

Additionally, the Rockefeller family also valued financial education from an early age. They believed that financial education was essential to maintaining family prosperity. As a result, they created a tradition of teaching their children and grandchildren the importance of money management and creating healthy financial habits.

One way the Rockefeller family maintained prosperity was through the creation of family foundations and businesses. They invested in various areas, such as oil, finance, and real estate, and always sought to diversify their investments to minimize risks.

Furthermore, they created a culture of financial planning and open communication within the family. Family members regularly met to discuss finances and investments, as well as working together on philanthropy projects.

The lesson we can learn from the Rockefeller story is that financial education and open communication are essential to maintaining prosperity in the family. By teaching the importance of money management and investing smartly from an early age, we can ensure that wealth is kept across generations. Additionally, philanthropy and social responsibility can be a way to give greater meaning to wealth, helping to build a lasting legacy.

Maintaining prosperity in the family is something many people aspire to achieve, but few know how to do so effectively. Prosperity is not just about money, but also about emotional well-being and quality of life. It is important for all family members to be in tune with each other and work together to achieve common goals. In this article, we will discuss some useful tips to help maintain prosperity in the family.

1. Open and Honest Communication

Communication is the key to maintaining harmony and prosperity in the family. It is important for all family members to communicate openly and honestly, without hiding anything from each other. It is important to discuss financial goals, such as saving money and investing in future projects. Everyone should be aware of the family's financial situation and monthly expenses.

2. Financial Planning

Having a financial plan is essential for maintaining prosperity in the family. It is important to create a family budget and stick to it. All expenses should be recorded and monitored regularly to ensure that the family is living within its financial means. Additionally, it is important to have an emergency fund to deal with unforeseen expenses.

3. Financial Education

It is important for all family members to be financially educated. This will help make more informed financial decisions and avoid financial problems in the future. Parents should teach children about money and finance from an early age, so that they can become financially responsible adults.

Teamwork

Prosperity in the family is achieved through teamwork. All family members should work together to achieve common financial goals. It is important for everyone to work together to save money, invest in future projects, and make important financial decisions.

4. Commitment and Discipline

Maintaining prosperity in the family requires commitment and discipline. It is important for all family members to be committed to achieving common financial goals and be disciplined enough to follow a financial plan. Everyone should be aware of their personal expenses and avoid unnecessary spending.

5. Professional Help

If the family is facing financial problems or needs help creating a financial plan, it is important to seek professional help. A financial consultant can help create a financial plan and advise on investments and other important financial matters.

Conclusion

Maintaining prosperity in the family requires open and honest communication, financial planning, financial education, teamwork, commitment, and discipline. It is important for all family members to work together to achieve common financial goals and be financially responsible. With these useful tips, the family can maintain prosperity and enjoy a healthy and prosperous financial life.

Chapter 19

Staying Committed to Your Financial Goals

One of the most inspiring examples of perseverance and commitment to financial goals is the case of Chris Reining, an American who was able to retire at 37 with a net worth of over one million dollars.

Chris worked hard from a young age and always knew he wanted to achieve financial independence. He worked early on to save money and invest wisely, always staying true to a strict budget. Chris was very conscious of his spending, avoiding waste and aggressively investing in low-cost index funds. He knew that time was one of his greatest allies in the pursuit of financial independence.

However, the path was not easy. Chris faced many obstacles along the way, such as the 2008 financial crisis, which severely affected his investments. He had to deal with the uncertainty and volatility of the financial market, but never lost sight of his long-term goals. In addition, Chris also had to deal with external expectations and pressures. Many friends and family members did not understand why he was so obsessed with money and early retirement. But he did not let himself be discouraged and remained firm in his convictions.

Today, Chris is a recognized writer and speaker in the field of personal finance. He shares his lessons learned along the way to help others achieve financial independence and build a more prosperous future. His story inspires many people to stay focused on their financial goals, even when the path seems difficult or uncertain.

Staying committed to your financial goals can be a challenge for many people, especially in a world full of distractions and spending temptations. However, it is essential to stay focused to achieve financial security and reach financial independence. In this chapter, I will discuss some tips to help you stay committed to your financial goals.

First, it is essential to set clear and specific financial goals. This may include things like saving for retirement, buying a house, or paying off debts. By having clear goals in mind, you will have a reference point to guide yourself and can evaluate your progress over time.

Second, it is important to create a budget and stick to it. A budget can help you control your spending and avoid spending money on unnecessary things. In addition, by maintaining a strict budget, you can save money and reach your financial goals more quickly.

Third, it is important to maintain the habit of saving regularly. This may include things like saving a fixed percentage of your income every month or saving any extra money you receive, such as a bonus or birthday gift. By maintaining the habit of saving regularly, you can reach your financial goals more quickly and avoid spending money on unnecessary things.

Fourth, it is important to avoid the temptation to spend money on things that are not essential. This may include things like impulse purchases, expensive dinners, or extravagant vacations. It is important to remember that while these things may be fun, they can prevent you from achieving your long-term financial goals. By avoiding the temptation to spend money on things that are not essential, you can stay committed to your financial goals.

Finally, it is important to find support in friends and family members who share your financial goals. Having a support group can help you stay motivated and committed to your financial goals, even when things get tough. In addition, sharing your financial goals with others can help you stay accountable and evaluate your progress over time.

In conclusion, staying committed to your financial goals can be a challenge, but it is essential to achieve long-term financial security and independence. Setting clear financial goals, creating a budget and sticking to it, maintaining the habit of regularly saving, avoiding the temptation to spend money on unnecessary things, and finding support in friends and family are some of the tips to help you stay committed to your financial goals. Remember that achieving your financial goals can be a slow process, but with commitment and dedication, you can achieve long-term financial security and independence.

Chapter 20

Conclusion: The journey to wealth and success.

There are several biblical passages that speak about finances and the importance of managing them wisely. One of them is the story of Joseph, son of Jacob, who was sold into slavery by his own brothers and eventually became the governor of Egypt.

Joseph faced many difficulties along his journey but always kept his faith in God and determination to achieve his goals. When he was sold into slavery, he ended up working for Potiphar, an Egyptian official, and thanks to his ability to manage the finances of the house, he became responsible for everything his master owned.

Unfortunately, Joseph was falsely accused by Potiphar's wife and ended up in prison. Even in prison, he continued to manage wisely and soon caught the attention of the jailer, who put him in charge of the other prisoners.

Over time, Joseph was called upon to interpret a dream of the Pharaoh, which predicted a period of seven years of abundance, followed by seven years of famine. Joseph, with his wisdom, suggested to the Pharaoh that during the years of abundance, Egypt stored enough grain for the years of scarcity, which ended up saving the Egyptian people from hunger.

Joseph was then appointed governor of Egypt, becoming one of the richest and most powerful people of his time. He used his wealth and influence to help his family, who had sold him into slavery years before, and to benefit the entire Egyptian people.

Joseph's story is an inspiring example of how determination, financial wisdom, and faith in God can lead a person to achieve financial success and help those around them. Joseph's journey shows that, even in moments of difficulty, it is possible to maintain perseverance and long-term vision, and that financial management can make a difference in the lives of many people.

The journey to wealth and success is an endeavor that requires much dedication, effort, and discipline. It is not an easy path, and there are often obstacles that need to be overcome. However, those who are committed to achieving their financial and personal goals are capable of overcoming these obstacles and achieving success.

One of the keys to the journey of wealth and success is financial education. It is important to have knowledge about finances, investments, and business strategies to make smart and informed decisions. This involves reading books, attending courses and seminars, and seeking guidance from financial professionals.

Furthermore, it is important to have a wealth mindset. This means believing that it is possible to achieve financial success and being willing to take calculated risks to achieve your goals. It also means avoiding limiting beliefs and working to overcome fears that may hinder success.

Another important aspect of the journey to wealth is charity and philanthropy. By sharing your resources with others, you can create a positive impact in your community and the world. This not only helps others but also brings personal satisfaction and a sense of purpose.

Maintaining commitment to your financial goals is essential to achieving wealth and success. This may involve setting clear goals and tracking your progress over time. It also means being disciplined with your finances, consistently saving and investing, and making smart financial choices.

The journey to wealth and success is a combination of financial education, wealth mindset, charity and philanthropy, and commitment to your financial goals. There is no one path to achieving wealth, but following these practices can help you achieve your personal and financial goals and enjoy a life of prosperity and fulfillment.

This book was written by Cristian Pontes with the intention of helping people achieve their financial goals and build a more prosperous life. I believe that everyone has the potential to achieve wealth and success as long as they have the right tools and knowledge. I hope this book is one of those tools for those seeking to improve their financial situation and achieve their dreams. Additionally, I believe that by helping people achieve their personal prosperity, I am also contributing to a better world, where more people are able to help their communities and create a positive impact on society. I believe that financial prosperity should not be viewed as a selfish goal, but rather as an opportunity to generate more abundance and share with those around us.

The author demonstrates an intense interest in studying and improving human beings in various aspects of life, from personal to professional. He is concerned with contributing to the improvement of the quality of life of less privileged communities. His passion for human development motivates him to seek knowledge and share his ideas and experiences. He believes that education is fundamental to building a more just and balanced society, and that everyone has a role to play in this transformation.

Cristian Pontes
Youtube Programa Chris Tattoo
Phone: 55-35-98423-6050